DECLUTTER Y

7 strategies to unfu*k yourself.

A step by step guide to learn to control your thoughts, stop worrying, relieve anxiety and eliminate panic attacks and negative thinking.

Mia Chandler

COPYRIGHT

indirectly. Respective authors own all copyrights not held by the publisher.

The information herein is offered for informational purposes solely and is universal as so. The presentation of the information is without contract or any type of guarantee assurance.

Table of Contents

Introduction

Do you frequently feel like there is too much going on in your life that keeping up with all of it is stressful and tiring? Are these happenings limiting your productivity levels to a point where you can't fulfill your otherwise normal routine? An examination of the cause of this problem that has faced you will reveal that you have so much baggage in your mind and life that it overwhelms you. What you need to do when this scenario arises is to declutter your mind. You need to get rid of the excess weighing you down and focus on what is important to you in your life.

You can make this possible for your life by decluttering. Decluttering your life is one of the key elements of a minimalist lifestyle.

Right now, minimalism is a lifestyle that everyone is yearning to achieve. It is a lifestyle that helps you get rid of all the unnecessary things that bring stress to your life.

As a minimalist, you dedicate your life to living on only what you need to live comfortably and keeping all the things that are not important to your life away from you.

You can take on too much in your life and barely have time to keep up with all of it. I was a victim of this way of living a few years back before minimalism saved me. Having a lot of work to do was a way of making myself feel important. I thought that if I wanted to make an impact in life, I needed to have many things going on at the same time in my life. This way, I would ensure that I had no time to lazy about and that I would be able to do a lot, at least that is what I thought.

I was taking on too much in my life that I had no time for myself. It was hard to keep up with everything, and after some time, I became a working robot. Everything I was doing was not personal to me anymore, I was doing it to get it done. This means that I was not giving it my all. I was not performing these tasks to the best of my ability; I was doing it to mark the task as complete. This was a disservice to myself because deep down, I knew that I could do better.

By taking on too much, I had no time to perfect my skills. So, all my work was just satisfactory and not well done. And with time, I was convinced that I was not good enough for anything.

I had categories of people in my head, those that are perfect at everything they do, and those that do not get things right. I would see myself in the latter group because of the number of times my work was sent back to me due to it being unsatisfactory.

It was when I had my encounter with the minimalism that I was able to know my worth. My first goal was to declutter my life and get rid of all my baggage.

In this writing, I am going to walk you through your decluttering journey. You will understand the importance of decluttering to your life and how to go about it to make it an enjoyable process.

From my decluttering journey, I realized that you could not declutter your whole life in a day. It is a journey that needs time and patience.

The first thing I suggest you do is to tune your mindset to understand that decluttering is good for you. When I started decluttering, I thought that the only way to do it was to dive in and go 'cold turkey.'

Well, was I wrong! I found myself connected to so many of my possessions and life routines. I started convincing myself that I needed them all, which did not help my decluttering process.

Then the process was tiring. Imagine sorting through so many boxes and other things in my house in one day... I was so exhausted, and my mindset was that decluttering is a brutal and tiring process that I will not be doing again.

I became negative about it, and all times I read and thought about it, my mind would take me back to how tired I was the previous time I tried it. And that was when I was decluttering my possessions. It was twice as hard when I

I was doing away with the extra activities in my life.

I found it impossible to let them go because they were what gave me a purpose in my life. I felt that letting go would mean I was not reliable anymore. That people would no longer count on me.

But I came to an understanding that decluttering is a process that requires patience and a good attitude. You cannot dive into it if your attitude is wrong.

I have tried decluttering with no patience and the wrong attitude, and I know how it negatively affects the whole cause, and this is not just a physical process but also an emotional one. I remember the self-talks I gave myself not to go and pick up something that I had gotten rid of. Everything in our lives has an emotional attachment to us. It is understandable when letting go of these items becomes hard.

This book is going to help you have an easy and fun decluttering experience. All the advice you will get from it will give you the strength you need to keep going and make sure you come out of this with only what you need to live comfortably.

Once I was done decluttering my life, I literally felt lighter. Nothing was wearing me down anymore. I was free to focus on myself and work on growing my skills. My mind always felt fresh, and I could now have clear thoughts and perform better.

The feeling is exciting. I can promise you that. I was now working on what I wanted, and I discovered many things about myself buried under all the baggage I previously had in my life.

The main improvement of decluttering is that it is going to give you your life back. As long as you are entertaining many things that are not important, you are not living your life for yourself. What you are doing is living your life to accommodate them. And decluttering will help you change that.

It will be living in vain if you do not live your own life by your own terms and discover your true potential. You have to do this for you now. Nobody will show you what you are capable of if you do not go out and find it for yourself. And you will not get it if you have a lot of things in your way keeping you from discovering yourself.

Have an open mind and the yearning to discover how this concept of decluttering will give you your life back as you read on. It is good that you have made this choice as a step to better your life. This book will be your guide, you will get useful tips and steps to declutter your life.

Chapter 1: Understanding the problems

At one point in their lives, everybody is concerned. Some individuals are persistent troublemakers. Worry is the primary component of both anxiety, depression, and disorders.

The problem with concern is that a solution is desperately needed. And to find a solution, you need to grasp it first.

Both of us have had worries, questions, and doubts. All of us have had feelings of confusion and tension about talking to a group of people, going to an interview, getting an operation, or beginning a new career.

Maybe you're worried about an upcoming event right now. You probably get worried when your partner is late home. If everything goes right-your, the partner arrives home, or the social event is postponed, the worry will vanish with it, but until it is over, the days or weeks leading up to it can be challenging.

Like other emotions, anxiety has three parts: thoughts, internal feelings, and habits. Let's take a closer look at each of the following functions.

Physical Nature

This aspect of worry entails the physical changes that happen in your body. In other words, the internal bodily changes you go through.

Some of the most popular physical signs of anxiety include:

Rapid breathing, which may make someone feel weak, shaky, and light-headed. Also, it may activate pins and needles in your toes and fingers.

Muscle tension, which activates tension within the jaw, headaches, tightness in your chest and throat.

A rush of hormones, which can generate hot flushes and make you sweat.

Diversities in the blood supply to your digestive system might trigger butterflies, sickness, and nausea.

It is easy for worry to go undiagnosed, especially if it reveals as a physical problem. For instance, stomach issues or an urgent need to go to the bathroom can always be the feeling of being anxious about a forthcoming event but might not be recognized.

While everyone has different thoughts when we are worried, we all experience similar physical responses. No matter the age, race, or gender, our bodies produce hormones that spread to various parts of the body when worried or scared. Adrenaline causes your heartbeat to increase, and the blood flows where it's needed.

The physical changes allow your body to protect you in a dangerous circumstance by running away or fighting. This is known as the flight or fight reflex.

This response is necessary to protect you against physical dangers. But, when there are no physical dangers, you don't need to run away, the impact of adrenaline decreases, and you might become agitated for a long time.

Behavioral Aspect

The behavioral aspect of anxiety involves the things you do or don't do when you feel worried. The same way each of us has different thoughts about a situation; everyone behaves differently.

If, for instance, you were worried before an exam, you might walk up and down the room. But someone else might sit and bite their nails as a result of anxiety. Someone else might resort to chewing gum.

When we feel worried, we act on different things, including what has activated the feelings of anxiety, our ability to control the situation, and how the situation compares to our past experiences.

Rather than respond by doing something, your behavior might entail not doing something. In the exam example, you might avoid it by failing to avail yourself of the day of the exam.

Therefore, when you feel worried, it will affect you physically, behaviorally, and cognitively. Let's assume that you were worried about speaking to a group of people. Below is how you might experience the worry.

Physical response: Increased pulse, rapid breathing, and stomach-churning.

Behavioral response. Playing with your pen and biting your nails.

Cognitive response. "I will stammer and not become clear, and everyone will think I'm not aware of what I am speaking."

There is not a single order by which the above properties of anxiety occur, but any other factor can impact the others: how you feel, act, and think are intrinsically related.

For instance, anxious response to addressing a group of people can start with a physical reaction: increased pulse, faster breathing, and hot flushes. This may activate a behavioral reaction where you play with your pen or bite your nails.

Or you might start to play with your pen and bite your nails. This may activate a physical response. And then your thoughts will follow.

Still, your anxious thoughts might start. These thoughts may then trigger increased pulse, hot flushes, and stomach-churning. Then you can begin to bite your nails and play with your pen.

To master how the following interaction of feelings, thoughts, and behaviors operate when you're worried, outline your own example of an event you always feel anxious about.

Cognitive Aspect

What you believe, your perceptions and interpretations of an upcoming event are part of the cognitive feature of worry.

Different people may hold different thoughts about the circumstances. For instance, in the example of sitting an exam, one person might be thinking, "I am not sure whether I can do this. I might be hopeless. I could fail. However, another person might be thinking, "Suppose I forget everything I have learned?" "What if they don't ask questions associated with the topics I have revised?"

Overall, what is always included in your thoughts and concerns about a given situation are the thoughts you might have concerning how you'll feel or act once you're experiencing that situation. You might say that you will:

Experience a heart attack and faint.

Lose control and go mad

Feel like things are moving so fast that you'll be separated from your environment and the people in it.

I want to run away and escape from the situation.

When you are anxious, you don't just think. You know and truly believe that you are hopeless, and you cannot do this.

When worry takes control of your life, you tend to believe that it will happen instead of accepting what might happen. This is referred to as 'cognitive fusion.' You experience your thoughts as a fact and a reality.

Self-Sustaining Property of Worry

Once you see, worry as thoughts, behavior, and physical feelings, it becomes easy to see how they are

interconnected and control you. You can also understand how anxiety can be self-sustaining. One property can feed another. For instance, the more worry you have, the more you might experience the physical feelings. This might then make you resort to unhelpful behaviors, which, in turn, make it possible to experience more worry.

You might, for instance, become worried about speaking in a public event. You become flustered and feel nauseous at the thought of being requested to speak in public. Then you become anxious about your worry showing and everyone learning that you're anxious. So you do whatever you can to skip meetings. But then you feel worried that your manager believes you have nothing to contribute, and you feel you need to work harder in other parts of your job to demonstrate that you've got something to contribute. Before you realize it, you will be trapped in a cycle of worry.

And in case you are scared about your worry and its symptoms, the feelings, behaviors, and thoughts- you might also acquire new anxieties or discover scenarios causing anxiety.

Is it Nature or Nurture?

Are you born to be worried, or do you 'learn' to be anxious?

It might be that some individuals are born sensitive and predisposed to anxiety and worry.

It might also be that you were not born anxious, but that feeling anxious might be something you learned early on in life. Close family members might have been worried and transferred their anxiety to you. Then you learned how to respond in the same way.

Past traumatic experiences, such as bullying, abuse, and domestic violence, can result in anxiety. If common childhood fears, such as a fear of the dark or a fear of being left alone, were not taken care of by my parents, the child might be more vulnerable to worry later in life. If you experienced many changes in your life when you were young, seeing your parents divorcing, being ill, or someone you love becoming ill, you might have been unsure about what would happen next. This might make you more vulnerable to worry.

If you experienced something distressing in the past, either as a child or an adult, and you struggled to control your emotions at the time, you might be anxious about the possibility of similar situations repeating in case they trigger the same feelings.

Some people can clearly identify a cause for their anxiety: a build-up of stress or having experienced a powerful life event such as losing their job or having surgery. It can be a current situation or several events or cumulative events that you consider stressful.

However, some people don't have an exact cause for their worry.

Anxiety, then, might be caused by one thing or various events. It could be that you were born predisposed to feeling anxious or that it's an effect of your upbringing, your current experiences. It could be a sequence of any of these factors.

However, there is a sum of forces in operation when you're anxious: physical feelings, thoughts, and behavior. And the following forces interact with each other. Learning this can help breakdown anxiety. It can help you better understand the aspect of anxiety-how and why it makes you feel, think, and act the way you do when you're worried.

The Main Causes of Worry

Past experiences are some of the causes which bring worry. Thieves may have stolen from you something in the street; therefore, you will be a bit worried when walking in the same street. You will always feel insecure about unpleasant things that happened to you. Always assure yourself that such occurrences will never occur, which is a means of fighting the attitude.

Low self-esteem could be another cause. You always believe whenever you do something, you always fail. You develop a negative perception and feel like something would be right if another person were to do it. This shows that you are undermining yourself, which is a bad thing, especially for people who are supposed to succeed. One should eliminate that fear of failure to believe that you can succeed regardless of the situation.

Sometimes an individual's economic and social aspects generate such vice in their body system. If one is from a humble background, you will likely experience this attitude when you face rich guys. You will be scared that they will judge you and despise you as they are above your status. The societal surroundings also affect this attitude because one's distanced when connecting with individuals of higher ranking. Think of how you would react if the president chose to visit your house? You will, for sure, get puzzled.

Your nature sometimes betrays you when one displays such character. Some people are normally bewildered or have unsettled actions. They display an irrational fear over something which cannot be established. Such nature can be inferred to the genetic makeup of that person. Additionally, if a person is a drug addict or has mental problems, they can show those emotions regularly.

Types of Worries

Any moment you experience unpredictable situations. For instance, in the business setting, you could experience the fear of investing your money in a particular investment. That is why there is a risk analysis in every business investment. In other words, this method of worrying can be handled at every angle. It causes someone to rethink their worrying nature and reflect on the necessary steps to take.

It's hard to fight a battle without learning what the struggle involves. Therefore, one has to understand the problems causing someone to panic. Excessive anxiety and worrying results in a disorder which familiar with your personality. Psychologists term this condition as mentally related. Some people fear to take part in certain activities because they believe their conscience alerts them of preceding failure. Simply put, this attitude is inferred by having the mental uneasiness of an object. To identify this condition fully, you must learn its different characteristics and types.

There is solvable anxiety, which is categorized and structured. This demonstration shows that one can extract its cause and the object related to the feeling. It is also considered authentic in the mental picture. Solvable worry or anxiety also contains a certain characteristic that one uses in resolving.

Structured feeling or worry is another type of concern. These emotions cannot be categorized, and one cannot understand their source or a specific subject of interest. Instances of a person getting naturally confused or experiencing personal disorders are some of those examples. You may ask why a certain person is anxious, but that person cannot clearly tell the reason for that behavior. Such situations require one to scrutinize their feelings for effective control.

Generalized anxiety disorder is another form that can be connected with your worrying nature. In this aspect, you cannot explain the real cause of that feeling. You experience physical nervousness and mental tension. Some people even consider that feeling as a warning sign of a likely absurd circumstance. When an individual feels uneasy about an event, that is a sign of an unpleasant event. The most common symptoms include fatigue, irritation, unclarified speed, and many others.

Some people find it difficult to speak in a public gathering. These are people who show irrational fear when connecting to the public. These people prefer to stay alone as they feel other people will judge or condemn them. They usually disvalue themselves and their social rankings. Such people are therefore distressed of being embarrassed. That nature is sometimes known as shyness. Working with shyness requires an individual to practice speaking to people or interact with them sufficiently.

Panic attacks are a strong worrying nature. Doubtless, at one point in your life, you experienced a rapid sense of nervousness and fear when you met something. Some people say they feel this reaction when they are sensing danger. Panic attacks can be defined as a personality disorder. It is a powerful and severe feeling that you can easily mistake it for a potential heart attack. Some of the following disorder symptoms consist of rapid heartbeat, trouble in breathing, excessive sweating, chest pain, or even numbness.

Do you know of individuals who dislike water because they are water phobic? If you have seen one, then this is another category of worried personnel. They are, hence the specific phobias that people normally have. These emotions are similar to an allergic reaction when one faces an object. Some people are scared of insects and other animals. For that reason, they worry when they meet them. Some symptoms of the above phobias consist of controlling excess fear, thus experiencing limitations in performing routine tasks.

There are situations where you experience posttraumatic disorders. These are unfavorable events in your life that caused sorrow and pain. These disorders preserve a scar in your life that you worry about when experiencing it. Imagine a lady who was once attacked in a certain location; any time she comes close to that place, she experiences strong panic.

Chapter 2: Identify Your Mind Enemy

There is a high possibility of experiencing sociopsychological problems if your vagus nerve is inflamed or damaged. These problems are mostly related to your psychological aspect and can only be noticed through your actions, and they initiated in your head as it depends on how your brain responds to different situations, so you need to understand the two systems of the vagus nerve continuously communicate with the brain, mainly about other body organs. The sympathetic nervous system is culpable for keeping you in action by feeding the cortisol and the adrenaline. In contrast, the parasympathetic nervous system is reliable while you are relaxed or resting.

In other words, the sympathetic system activates actions while the parasympathetic decelerates actions and keeps you at rest. However, the latter utilizes acetylcholine as neurotransmitters that control the blood pressure and heart rate to create a perfect relaxation condition. As a part of the body's autonomous nervous system, the vagus nerve may fail or experience damage hindering its full potential to the body. The most common condition that affects the vagal nerve is inflammation that makes it malfunction. This condition could worsen the whole body's functioning as the vagal nerve facilitates essential processes that keep the body healthy and kicking.

Chronic stress

The problem is associated with overthinking things that might be beyond your control. Stress can also be a result of issues in your vagal nerve. For instance, when your body is exposed to harmful situations, it releases chemicals meant to respond appropriately and avoid injury. As noted before, the sympathetic nervous system stimulates the response through the fight-or-flight reaction, and it is at this time, your heart rate increases to quickly supply blood to the rushing body parts and muscles. The response likewise enhances the quickened inhalation of oxygen to assist in blood oxygenation. In this case, stress acts as a protective mechanism that your body initiates to keep you alert and out of danger.

There are different perceptions of stress among people. In other words, what causes stress for one person might be of little concern to the other, and people have different ways and potential to deal with it. This means that if stress is meant to prevent you from danger, it should not be treated as a bad thing. Besides, our bodies have a unique mechanism that is intended to deal with specific doses of stress. However, the body's capabilities could weaken as you may be overwhelmed by chronic stress resulting from vagal nerve inflammation or damage. This type of stress impacts almost every aspect of your life, including physical health and emotions. Chronic stress is also characterized by low esteem where you feel worthless and not comfortable while in public.

If you are suffering from chronic stress, you will feel overwhelmed and easily agitated by others. As a result, you end up avoiding interactions with your peers as you feel they want to control you. Avoiding people and having low self-esteem makes you suffer in isolation as you may not realize the seriousness of the condition. With this in mind, chronic stress's emotional symptoms could end up being a serious condition if not detected and treated. Consequently, your judgment becomes impaired by the condition as you get prone to the inability to focus and forgetfulness. You also remain pessimistic and unable to positively view your life and exhibit nervousness through fidgeting and nail-biting behaviors.

First, people with chronic stress seem to avoid complex responsibilities. They also experience sudden changes in your appetite, where they either eat excessively or not eat at all. Second, procrastination is also associated with chronic stress, and you could be at risk of indulging in alcohol and drug abuse. Therefore, you should ask for feedback if you think that you are suffering from stress. A doctor will usually record the observations and what you report to come to a proper conclusion about the condition you are suffering from. In this case, the underlying cause of chronic stress is a dysfunctional vagus nerve, so you should take the necessary measures to ensure that you start vagal verve treatment to normalize its functionality.

Anxiety and Panic Attacks

Whenever you come across a stressful situation, the body activates the vagus nerve's sympathetic nervous system. In most cases, the system is reversed once the situation is over. However, the persistence of the tension would mean that the vagus nerve's sensitive effect would be prolonged until you are out of harm's way. The effect is usually triggered and ended by a physiological response in your body, but a prolonged fight-or-flight response would cause your body problems. The situation would lead to the activation of the intestine and the adrenal axis of the brain. As a result, the brain increases hormones that travel through the bloodstream to stimulate adrenaline and cortisol induction.

The hormones act as inflammatory precursors and immune suppressors, causing the anxiety that could make you ill and depressed, so the chronic anxiety increases the production of glutamate in the brain, which, when combined with cortisol, reduces the hippocampus in charge of memory retention. The worsening of this situation leads to the development of anxiety disorder characterized by panic attacks. The problem is characterized by a sense that you are in impending danger, or your life is at risk. These false signs may be frequent, depending on the seriousness of the condition. You feel afraid of losing your valuables or as if you are about to die with this condition. In most cases, the effect seems uncontrollable as the panic creates an illusion that it has been decided elsewhere.

At this time, your heart rate is increased due to the tension, making it pound on your chest as your breath goes wild. The blood pressure increases as the body take it as an attack. These panic attacks might confuse your body as they give false alarms making your body sweat as if you are in a serious situation even though you may be lying on your couch. The helplessness associated with anxiety and panic attacks leaves you trembling with fear of imagined imminent danger, and you will realize that your body is shaking uncontrollably due to a perceived situation.

The quickened breathing associated with anxiety makes your throat experience fast air movement as the lungs try to suck as much air as possible to supply to the heart, resulting in experiencing tightness in your throat and a burning effect. You may also fall short of breath as the heart rate increases and experience prolonged chills if you suffer from anxiety and panic attacks. These chills could be against the sweating and heat produced by the body as your adrenaline keeps you in the fight-or-flight reaction. This problem makes you look confused and unaware of the immediate environment.

The condition should be taken in all seriousness as it could lead to suicidal thoughts and actions as the victim sees no other way out. This is because the body's experiences are severe and complicated and would require immediate treatment to avoid causing accidents and incidents. The hot rashes experienced in this problem are experienced in the neck, chest, or stomach and are indications that the body is at the full alert of the faced danger. Generally, these illusions make the person feel detached from the real world, and it would be hard to communicate with them when under panic attacks. In other words, their mind takes them to the world where they see a danger in every corner. The total panic is so real that the person continually experiences a tingling and numb sensation.

Other anxieties and panic attacks include headache, chest pain, and dizziness, especially after the attack is over. During this time, the victim relaxes and tries to recover lost energy, but with chronic panic attacks, the victim worries that the experience may happen again. They also feel uncomfortable associating with others and attending public functions as they are wary of possible attacks. At this time, the body exerts these symptoms due to the confusion caused by the dysfunctional vagus nerve, so if you experience these symptoms, you should see a doctor check on your vagus nerve's condition and take the necessary measures.

Phobias

Vagal inflammation is known to cause phobias as one of the sociopsychological problems in the human body. Mostly, the problem is characterized by a deep sense of panic and irrational fear reaction. When you are in this condition, you encounter different fear sources, depending on how you perceive the environment. In some instances, you could be experiencing phobia in specific situations, objects, or places. This form of vagal nerve damage is known to complicate how your brain interprets some aspects of the environment, so you end up feeling insecure in dark or quiet environments, especially if you have had a frightening experience before.

The effects of phobia vary depending on the seriousness and the body's mechanism to repair damaged tissues. These conditions determine the impact of phobia in your body as it could only be an annoying experience or build up to a severe and disabling. If you experience phobia, you might be helpless about it as it is caused by other underlying conditions such as vagal nerve inflammation. Therefore, you are prone to stress as you always remain afraid of a possible attack, making you unproductive and unsocial, especially in the workplace. The condition may be different from one person to the other, hence the different categorization according to the

trigger and symptoms.

One common type of the condition is agoraphobia, which is characterized by the panic of situations and places that you cannot escape from. People who have agoraphobia are mostly afraid of being in open places such as outside their houses or in crowded places. People feel uncomfortable while in social areas and like to spend most of their time indoors. The main reason why these people avoid public places is due to the anxiety of experiencing phobia publicly, which might embarrass them and leave them helpless. In some cases, people with agoraphobia may experience a health emergency, making them remain in places where they could ask for an urgent response.

Social phobia has relatively similar characteristics and is also known as social anxiety disorder combined with anxiety symptoms. As the name suggests, the victims of this disorder avoid social places and prefer staying in isolation for fear of humiliation and discrimination if they become phobic. This type of phobia is so serious as it could be caused by a simple interaction, such as answering a phone call or talking to a stranger. It makes the victims go out of their way to avoid these interactions making life hard for them, especially if they are working or attending school. A phobia may be triggered by a specific object, with common categories being the environment, medical, situations, or animals.

In this case, you experience phobia after experiencing environmental conditions such as storm or lightning, while an animal phobia results from encountering animals such as rodents or snakes. In medical phobia, you feel threatened by the sight of blood or syringe. These experiences are hard to live with, and you should take the necessary steps to ensure that the condition is controlled to help you live happily and fearlessly. The problem is characterized by uncontrollable anxiety, especially when you experience a source of fear. You may also find yourself doing extra lengths to ensure that you avoid perceived sources of concern, even if it means changing direction. If you are affected by this problem, you are likely to be unproductive in your workplace as you could not function properly when the source of fear is around.

It will be hard to control the feeling even after realizing that the fear is exaggerated, unreasonable, and irrational. Some of the physical effects of phobia include trembling and abnormal breathing. At this time, the body is accelerating blood and chemicals' supply to the body to tackle the perceived threat. There is confusion and disorientation as you remain stuck between understanding the danger and taking swift action to get out of danger. The accelerated heartbeats are likely to cause abnormal breathing, which could lead to pain in the chest as the lungs try to grasp as much oxygen as they can. The best remedy for this condition would be to understand the underlying cause and seek medical help to repair and heal the damaged vagus nerve.

Bipolar disorder

The problem is also caused by vagal dysfunction and inflammation and was formerly referred to as a manic depression. It is a mental condition that triggers a moody feeling and swinging emotions. When the emotions are high, they are referred to as mania or hypomania, and depression when they are low. If you are depressed, you probably will experience hopelessness, sadness, and lost pleasure and interest. The feeling makes you hate activities you liked before and lose interest in meeting the people you love. However, the feeling is sometimes short-lived as you may suddenly experience high moods that make you feel euphoric and irritably full of energy.

The drastic mood changes significantly affect how you behave, judge, or sleep. It also hinders you from clear reasoning and making the right decision. There are numerous episodes of these mood swings that occur several times annually. In some cases, you may experience changes in events and emotional symptoms, while others may not experience them at all. The condition is manageable through the follow up of a treatment plan that includes counseling and medication. When a dysfunctional vagus nerve causes the condition, it could only be treated by healing the nerve. Several types of this disorder include depression and hypomania. These symptoms could cause drastic life effects and significant distress if left unaddressed.

Bipolar disorder is experienced when the condition triggers a break from reality and makes you fear your imagination. It is characterized by a single manic episode and occurs either before or after the incident. Bipolar II is defined by a major depressive disorder lasting weeks, followed by a hypomanic episode lasting about a week. The condition is more common in women but is also experienced by men. In cyclothymia, you experience depression and hypomania bouts, which are relatively shorter than those caused by the last two types. Additionally, the condition is characterized by a month or two for stability when the problem recurs and extends for some weeks. The mania and hypomania episodes are distinct in their symptoms, but the mania episode is more severe and is known to cause problems in public places such as workplaces or schools.

The condition also affects your relationship with your peers and family as it distances you from the reality hence the need to take drastic measures to curb it. The mania and hypomania episodes are characterized by jumpy and abnormal upbeats where you remain restless and agitated by things that might be perceived or out of control. The condition increases your activities as you seem to have extra energy to perform various tasks. These episodes make you feel overconfident and a sense of well-being, assuring you that you can succeed in everything you try and that you are perfect. The euphoria could lead to embarrassment as you try to prove your point. You run out of control in whatever you do as you seem to take over your company's management or want to replace the monitor in your class.

You may always remain and uncontrollably talkative and seem excited about topics that could be boring to your audience. Bipolar disorder keeps your body engaged, hence the talkativeness and overreaction to minor things. Your thoughts also remain at a high rate as they think about things that could be out of the world. The increased interest in uncommon things could make you lose interest and easily diverted to other topics, so you quickly lose interest and remain unpredictable on the issues that you would address. The major depressive episodes cause noticeable difficulties in your daily activities, with most psychological symptoms. The effects could make you lose or gain weight as you suffer from swing appetite. The feeling of worthlessness associated with this disorder could lead to inappropriate guilt. If you suffer from this condition, you are likely to have difficulties thinking or concentrating with a high possibility of developing suicidal thoughts. For that reason, you should understand the underlying cause of the condition and take drastic measures to address it. With the healing of the vagal nerve, you are sure to regain your consciousness and suppress the disorder.

Chapter 3: Why Do We Have Negative Thoughts?

Overthinking happens when the brain becomes too caught up with certain thoughts, thus causing the person to act upon the said thoughts. It is essentially a mental state wherein the brain is trapped in repeated analysis over the same topic or issue.

As a result, energy is expended unnecessarily, while signs of mental strain begin manifesting in the individual's day-to-day activities and even in one's interactions with other people.

To better demonstrate how the brain works when it is engaged in overthinking, go through the following list of scenarios—some of which may even sound familiar to you:

You cannot stop thinking about a personal problem or an event that has already transpired. Rather than focus on how to solve your current predicament, you cannot seem to pull yourself away from these thoughts. No matter what you do, your thinking keeps coming back to the problem or the event itself—not what you can do to get yourself out of this situation.

Something terrible has happened to you. As a result, you cannot seem to stop asking yourself why that has happened to you. You also find yourself ruminating about what would have happened instead if only you had done things a little differently.

Your mind jumps to the worst conclusions, even without any solid or sound basis at all. It has been occurring to your regularly so that, by now, the negative thoughts appear to be following some pattern in your head.

You find yourself obsessing about the tiny details in your day-to-day experiences, especially when it involves interacting with those around you.

You even come up with dialogues in your head, recreating mentally certain life events you think you could have done better.

You assign meaning to every word, thought, and action that sometimes goes beyond reasonable and realistic. People also say that you read into things, only to realize that they are not worth your time and effort.

If you picture yourself in any of those cases, and if you think that such scenarios happen to you frequently, then you might be falling into the habit of overthinking.

As shown in the examples above, addressing this issue is of the utmost importance. Overthinking is keeping you from moving forward and experiencing new things in life. It is like having your hand-tied with a rope that is attached to a pole. You can only go around in circles around the same thing, over and over again.

What Overthinking Is and Isn't it?

Right off the bat, it should be made clear that overthinking is not a form of mental illness. It is, however, a common symptom that can be observed among different types of anxiety disorders.

For example, Ben has been diagnosed with panic disorder. He is prone to overthink about when the next panic attack might happen. If he thinks something might trigger an attack, he cannot help himself but obsess over this possibility as such, his tendency to overthink these triggers only serves to increase the risk of panic attacks.

You do not have to be suffering from an anxiety disorder to engage in overthinking. This is an all-too-common human experience that happens almost naturally to everyone.

You may feel concerned over what you have said to your friend the last time you talked over the phone. Perhaps, you are worried about an upcoming test or job interview. You might feel a little too conscious about how others perceive you at work. These are just some examples of common scenarios where overthinking is at play.

It should also be noted that there is a distinction between the two forms of overthinking:

Brooding Over The Past

Dwelling about the mistakes you have done, and the opportunities you have missed out on can be detrimental to your current happiness and mental state.

Worrying About The Future

The unpredictability of what could happen next can trap a person into a never-ending cycle of "what-ifs" and "should-I's."

Overthinking is also different from introspection. The latter involves gaining personal insights and fresh personal perspectives about a certain matter. You introspect with a clear purpose in mind.

On the other hand, overthinking involves negative feelings about things that are usually outside of your control. As such, you will not feel like you have progressed at all after engaging in overthinking.

Causes of Overthinking

There is no single origin or trigger for one to engage in overthinking. It can be born out of genuine worry for one's welfare and those of others. Some overthink how they have been conditioned to think by their parents, their teachers, and their peers.

Extreme forms of overthinking are believed to be rooted in certain mental and psychological issues that a person is suffering from. These include but are not limited to:

post-traumatic stress disorder (PTSD); panic disorder; social anxiety disorder; substance-induced anxiety disorder; separation anxiety disorder; different types of phobias, particularly agoraphobia; and physical, mental, and/or emotional trauma.

Linking mental health issues with overthinking, however, is not as straightforward as it may seem. Some experts suggest that overthinking contributes to the decline of one's mental health. However, others are reporting that existing mental health problems can trigger a person to engage in overthinking.

Therefore, giving a definitive answer on the actual cause of overthinking can get you stuck in a loop. The actual case may also vary from one individual to another.

Rather than ruminate over the exact origin of overthinking, it would be best if you focused instead on learning how to assess yourself for signs of overthinking. Through this, you will be able to check if your tendency to overthink is getting out of hand already.

Signs You Are Being Controlled by Overthinking

Much like any human behavior, the effects of overthinking can be described as a dichotomy.

On one end, overthinking may be considered helpful since it allows a person to learn from past experiences and prevent the recurrence of certain mistakes in the future. When used in this way, overthinking can be beneficial in terms of problem solving and decision-making.

The problem begins when these thoughts become excessive, thus creating anxiety, stress, and a sense of fear and dread within the person. At this point, overthinking has gone beyond simply thinking too much about a person or a thing—overthinking has become an obsession that disrupts an individual's capacity to function and interact with other people.

If you are experiencing at least one of the following situations, then it's evident that you are being controlled by overthinking:

Continually measuring your worth, success, and happiness against the people around you;

Focusing on the worst possible outcomes whenever you or someone you care for is involved in something risky or dangerous;

Having trouble in keeping up with and contributing to conversations because you go over your potential responses for too long that either you miss the appropriate timing for your responses, or the conversation itself has already ended;

Worrying about future activities and task that you must accomplish so much that you feel overwhelmed at just the thought of having to do any of them;

Repeatedly thinking about personal mistakes and failures from the past, thus preventing you from moving on with your life;

Repeatedly reliving past trauma, loss, or abusive situation that robs you of your chance to cope with it;

Failing to calm down your racing thoughts and overwhelming but vague emotions that seemingly manifest out of nowhere.

Please note that the signs of overthinking, as highlighted above, are not exhaustive. However, if you find yourself continuously thinking about certain aspects of your life, or you find yourself in an endless cycle of non-productive thoughts, then that in itself is a sign that you are embroiled in overthinking.

Effects of Overthinking on You

No matter how similar the circumstances are between two people, their respective manner of overthinking would not be the same. As such, the effects of overthinking would be felt differently by each individual.

However, psychologists observed that those who cannot control their tendency to overthink suffer from a decreased quality of life. To give you a background on the possible effects of overthinking in your life, here are some common examples of difficulties faced by those who have been identified as chronic over-thinkers:

Making new friends or keeping the ones they already have can be tough due to their struggles in effectively communicating their thoughts and feelings.

They find it hard to go out and have fun doing their hobbies because they have already spent their time and energy ruminating about certain matters inside their heads.

Setting up appointments or even simply going to the store can be an arduous task for them.

Taking and exercising full control of their thoughts and emotions seem impossible because their mind is already strained and overworked.

Looking through these points, you can surmise that overthinking can ruin your relationships, isolate you from the rest of the world, and it can increase your risk of developing other serious mental issues, such as depression and anxiety disorder.

The bottom line is that overthinking has wide-reaching effects in almost everything you do and want to do in life. It not only limits you but also on those who wish to express their support to you. This means that overthinking can create serious problems in your personal abilities and the kind of relationships you will have.

There is actually no single type of care that you can adopt to completely relieve yourself of overthinking and its negative effects on you. Perhaps, one day, the mental health community would be able to develop the ultimate solution for this.

However, this should not stop you from seeking out methods that can help you control your thoughts and eliminate your tendency to overthink. This book shall help you understand and apply the strategies that would work best for you, given your situation's peculiarity.

Case Study

Amy is a middle-school teacher who frequently found herself worried about what people thought of her and how people see her worth as a teacher. Whenever she interacted with a parent or a co-teacher, she would usually pause for a second or two to determine if her words were appropriate or offensive.

At times, Amy would be filled with dread as question upon question began flooding her head. She would attempt to answer all of them, but doing so did not alleviate the stress and discomfort.

When her overthinking began affecting her work quality, Amy decided that it is time to find a way out of the miserable recurring situation. She did not, however, want to settle for a short-term solution.

What Amy wanted was to find a way to stop overthinking for good. She had admitted to herself that something was wrong and that serious steps must be taken as soon as possible. This acknowledgment by itself was a huge step towards her goal.

Practice Test

If you have a similar goal with Amy, you need to take a moment and recognize the effects of overthinking in your life. This will be part of your motivation to pursue your goal to overcome overthinking.

In your personal journal, describe specific incidents in the following key areas of your life where your incessant thoughts have taken over your good sense.

a.   Family

b.   Friendship

c.   Romantic Relationship

d.   Work

e.   Health and Fitness

Then, answer the following questions right after your responses for each area:

What do you think triggered you to engage in overthinking?

How did it make you feel at the time?

How do you feel about that incident now?

Anxiety, Negative Thought, and Worry

Anxiety is wherein an individual suffers from uncontrollable negative thoughts and excessive feelings of worry. Some people also experience physical symptoms of anxiety, such as chest pains and trembling.

There is no single cause that triggers anxiety, negative thought, or worry. Experts suggest that these feelings originate from various factors, including genetics and one's external environment.

What is clear at this point is that certain emotions, experiences, and instances can bring out or even worsen anxiety symptoms. These factors are referred to as triggers.

What Triggers These Feelings?

Triggers of anxiety, negative thought, and worry vary from one person to another. However, these triggers can be categorized into their probable sources, such as:

Romantic Relationships

Relationships are a landmine of potential triggers for anxiety, negative thought, and worry. Even when a couple is just at the start of their relationship, the novelty of being together with another person can put a strain on one's mental and emotional health.

Having arguments or disagreements with one's partner can be particularly stressful at any point in the relationship. If the couple is not effective communicators, the lack of conflict resolution between them may trigger feelings.

Family Matters

You cannot choose your family, so even when they make you feel upset or unhappy, it is nearly impossible to cut them off from your life completely. As a result, spending time with them may cause you to feel elevated anxiety levels and increased negative thoughts.

Becoming a parent is frequently one of the biggest life milestones that a person can have. Even though it is most exciting, this entails the new responsibilities that can trigger many people.

They may experience doubts about whether or not they will make good parents. Some are also worried about the strain that will cause their career, social life, and personal finances.

Friendships

Much like your romantic relationships, your friendships may trigger your anxiety, especially when you disagree with your friends. You may also begin harboring negative thoughts about them if you fail to communicate with them effectively. Worrying about the future of your friendship with them would then be a common thing, especially when you begin questioning yourself if you should stay friends with them.

Jobs and Career

Your current job and career may cause you to feel these things, especially when you do not enjoy what you are doing. Forcing yourself to work for something that is not your true calling can lead you further into a boring, depressing, and unfulfilled life.

Money

Financial worries, such as paying off a debt or saving up money, are commonly felt by people who suffer from these feelings. Unexpected bills and sudden financial instability have also been identified as strong triggers for many individuals.

Loss

Loss is often associated with intense feelings of sadness, regret, and fear. An individual who has recently experienced the loss of a loved one may feel anxious about what their life would be from then on. They may also have negative thoughts about the circumstances that have led to the said loss. Some may even feel particularly worried that they will never recover from their grief and that they will never feel normal again.

Trauma

Whether they are physical, verbal, or sexual, personal traumas are particularly harrowing experiences for anyone. They tend to have long-lasting effects, especially when the person cannot help but relieve that specific moment in his/her head over and over again.

Health Issues

Receiving an unexpected and/or upsetting diagnosis, especially when it pertains to serious chronic illnesses, can trigger one's anxiety, negative thought, and worry.

Because it is deeply personal, the after-effects of receiving such news are usually intensely felt by the individual.

Many people report having more than one trigger for their anxiety, negative thoughts, and worries. Some experience anxiety attacks with no apparent trigger.

Because of this, you must assess yourself and find out what may trigger these feelings within you. After doing that, you're going to be able to manage them better later on.

Chapter 4: How to Develop a Positive Thinking

Positive Thinkers Handle Stress Way Better

Have you ever been at work and got a notice that your manager needs to see you, and so you've been thinking all day about what the meeting could mean? Maybe you failed somewhere. Maybe you've done some terrible things which you have forgotten. Or maybe a terrible story about you has spread like wildfire, and you're supposed to defend yourself. So the next few hours before the meeting, you run over every possible negative reason for the meeting. Your mind is cloudy. You are trapped in your own anxiety. Then the meeting finally arrives, and you discover that you forgot to submit some paperwork. The stress you experienced the whole day was irrelevant, and therefore a massive amount of your precious emotional energy was wasted. Most of our daily stress-just, like in the following scenario, is self-created.

Research reports that stress itself doesn't exist in an event, but instead in our thoughts of an event. In other words, regardless of what takes place in life, you have the ability to sit in the emotional driver's seat. Pessimists normally approach commonplace life situations with the mind that they have committed a mistake. In the preceding example, many people constantly assume that the only reason a boss should ever call us is that we've committed a mistake. This thinking not only generates extra stress but denies us opportunities and friendships, and it can impact our ability to control stress in the long-term. On the other hand, optimists do not adopt sentiment based on a given situation until all the facts required to examine it fairly are available. This doesn't mean that the optimist imagines that something amazing will take place at the meeting. They're not sitting waiting anxiously, counting down the hours until their office time so they can receive a bigger prize. They're just not assuming anything at all.

In case the event is negative, the positive individual benefits from the fact they haven't been mulling over every possibility and developing million-and-one negative situations in their head. This makes them ready to control the situation's results, less likely to overreact to pent-up emotion, and able to resolve any troubles that they are faced with. Therefore, positive people are problem-solvers and depend on handling skills rather than venting on the problem at hand.

Know from today that you have a choice to make where you invest your energy. Remember that most of the stress in your daily life can be avoided or even reduced by maintaining a positive attitude. Research shows that optimists not only create less stressful situations but also go through less stress than pessimists. As you become more optimistic, you will start to let go of negative events more quickly. This prevents stressful situations from increasing and becoming overwhelming.

You will also manage to establish a better support system because you have stopped to assume the worst about every situation you enter. When stressful situations pop up, you should manage to reach out to your friends and depend on them to help you. When you begin to see the good things, you have better relationships and less stress. Therefore, you can let go of some of your unnecessary baggage. I believe you agree that the world can use a few more people who leave their baggage at home.

Positive Thinking is Necessary for Your Health

The Mayo Clinic discovered that negative thinking could activate your need for medical care, as well as increase your probability of heart disease. To demonstrate how powerful positive thinking and behaviors can change your health, below are three studies on how positivity impacts health.

As part of a study at the University of Missouri, students performed positive journaling every day three times a week. After three months, the students reported better moods and had fewer health center visits than those who did not journal.

A study of post-operative breast cancer patients performed by Indiana University discovered that those who lived a positive life experienced less of natural killer cells, a form of white blood cells that can destroy tumor cells. These cells are necessary for the long-term healing process, meaning a positive lifestyle enabled post-op patients with a strong immune system.

Researchers from John Hopkins University monitored a group of people with family histories of heart diseases for twenty-five years. Over that research period, members who lived a positive lifestyle reported a one-third decrease in a heart attack.

These are only a limited part of the hundreds of articles that connect a cheerful disposition with better long-term health. The main lesson is that optimists experience less pain, have increased heart function, longer lifespan, and a stronger immune system. It should be noted that a positive person doesn't imply you get obsessed over living a good healthy lifestyle. In fact, deciding to live your life on the sunny side of the street will cause you to make healthier life choices.

Simple methods to improve your health with positivity

1.   Maintain a daily journal of positive things taking place in your life.

2.   Take a brief walk around your neighborhood and smile at the people you pass.

3.	Every time you find yourself in front of a mirror, say something positive to yourself.

4.	Call someone you love and tell them how you value them.

Positivity Will Make You More Resilient

Many people believe that resilience is a personality trait: you're either born with it or not. However, I believe that it's actually a dynamic learning process, and the research tends to support this. The more positive you are about yourself, the more you cannot sweat the small stuff, and the better you will make it through the big scary, heart-pounding stuff. You must learn to analyze situations logically in times of stress and place whatever crazy event you're going through in the context of the bigger picture. This will allow you to remain concentrated and enable you to understand the entire situation's actual need versus the disastrous story that unmitigated shock automatically reminds you are going on.

Also, even in the saddest, and most devastating situations, there's always a silver lining. Taking advantage of skills such as self-assessment and problem-solving, you have the chance to learn and grow from every negative circumstance rather than concentrate on how disastrous the situation is turning your life in the short-term. When you do this, every stumbling block becomes a chance to grow and change.

Better resilience isn't just as simple as focusing on the bright side when bad things occur. Let's say I am having a great day. I will notify my best friends and perhaps my parents. Maybe mentioning it in a conversation with others if it pops up, but it's just a brief mention. Alternatively, if I experience a bad day, I will tell everybody. I will mention every single detail; what people are wearing, the appearance on their faces, what the cafeteria was offering that day. I could even provide sound effects to demonstrate the terror of it all.

How to Develop a Positive Look

Monitor positive things that occur in your life in a spreadsheet. When stressful situations happen, you will have a list of positive things in your life to draw on to push you through.

Practical Tips to Help You Attain a Positive Mindset

The power of positive thinking is a common idea, and sometimes it can look like a cliché. However, several research tests have demonstrated the physical and emotional benefits of positive thought. A positive mindset provides you with a lot of confidence, good mood and helps reduce the chances of suffering from depression and other stress-related problems.

Well, we can refer to it as positive imagery or general optimism for those who don't know what positive thinking is, but these are still general concepts. If you want to learn how to think positively, you will need deep examples to guide you through the process.

1. Start your day with a positive statement

The way you begin your day sets the tone for the entire day. Have you ever woken up late, panicked, and thought like nothing good happened the rest of the day? This could be because you started the day with a negative emotion and pessimistic perception that translated into every other event you experienced. Rather than allow this to continue, start your day with positive affirmations. Face the mirror as talk to yourself, even if you feel stupid. You will be shocked at how much your day changes.

2. Identify humor in bad situations

Allow yourself to experience humor even in the most difficult situations. Tell yourself that this situation will probably turn out to be a good story later and try to crack a joke about it.

3. Focus on the good things, no matter how small they are

Of course, you're going to face obstacles throughout the day. There's never a perfect day. When you face such a challenge, concentrate on the benefits, regardless of how small they seem. For instance, if you're stuck in traffic, think about the amount of time you have to listen to the rest of your best podcast.

4. Keep away from negative people

Negative people can be a major headache to thinking positively. They can trigger anxiety and self-doubt. Sometimes, it can be described as crowd-mentality, so don't fall victim to it.

The actions of negative people will eventually affect your behavior. If you want to be more confident and positive, it is important to select friends wisely. Choose individuals who not only speak with confidence and positivity but demonstrate those qualities.

5. Concentrate on the present

Forget what your boss said five minutes ago. Forget whatever he might say five minutes from now. Concentrate on this moment. In most cases, you will realize it's not as bad as you thought. Most sources of negativity arise from the memory of a recent event of a possible future event. Remain in the present moment.

6. Transform failures into lessons

You are not perfect. You're going to commit mistakes and experience failure in multiple jobs and contexts. Rather than concentrate on how you failed, consider what you're going to do the next time. Transform your failure into a lesson.

7. Think of the repercussions

For instance, if you have a deadline for a particular assignment, and it becomes clear that you're not going to meet it, think of what might happen. If you complete it on time, it will not be as good as you expected. If you spend more time, it might result in other problems.

This is the best time to ask yourself whether your negative thinking is generated by perfectionism. It is either important not possible to be perfect. The best thing you can do is to do the best job that you can do. Virtually, it is possible to keep changing something, but you have to request whether the improvements that would be realized are significant for the long term results of delaying competition.

Again consider the solutions. For example, you can request an extension to the deadline, or you might be able to delegate some of the work. There are usually different options available. By taking advantage of the repercussions, you can remain positive and in control.

Chapter 5: Minimalist Mindset

Minimalism isn't living in a sterile, dull, monotone environment. In fact, it is the opposite. The way you create your minimalist life depends entirely on you and your priorities. The underlying philosophy behind minimalism is to bring you more financial, emotional, material, and physical clarity and freedom. When you make space for the truly relevant things and people in your life, all other areas will start to follow as well.

People who are not familiar with a minimalist lifestyle will often see it as extreme or fringe. But once you realize and become aware that you don't need excess material things to make you fulfilled and happy, it's not even close to radical. It's simple. It's the ability to live a simple life and find meaning and joy in the things you prioritize.

Some people embrace change, and their transition to a minimalist lifestyle is easy, and they get used to it quickly. There are also people whose adjustment to change takes time and effort. So, the answer to this question is something you'd have to estimate according to your personality. If this lifestyle suits you and you feel lighter and better because of it, you're sure to get used to it and enjoy it.

Here are some key reasons to embrace minimalism:

- Your possessions will no longer own you. Instead, you'll learn how to select which ones are necessary and essential and which are just mere clutter;

- You'll gain a sense of freedom and liberation from the pressures of "modern" life. You'll understand that success comes from within – from your feeling of fulfillment and not having an enormous home, several cars, comfortable clothes, jewelry, or social status.

- You'll spend less money. And that's a good thing. Spending less on things you don't need means saving pay for things you do need. And that's called financial freedom.

- You'll feel more productive. Decluttering your mind, life, and home, as well as your working space, can contribute significantly to productivity. All the energy that comes with an over-stuffed place will go away, and a new, fresh one will take its place. It'll bring you positivity, fresh ideas, and a feeling of openness and will-power.

- You'll learn not to get attached emotionally to material objects. Instead, use that energy to connect with the people you love. That's way better for your well-being than any item you'd buy.

- The reduction is the keyword when adopting a minimalist lifestyle. Expect to reduce significantly the number of items that you and your family own. These will be items that are not crucial for surviving and living – mostly; they're items that you bought as an impulse purchase, things you keep "just in case" you ever need them, things you buy in bulk so that you're never out of something and basically, anything extra. This creates room for air, energy, and essential elements.

• You'll have more time to assign to your hobbies, family, and health. This is one of the best benefits of the minimalist lifestyle – your time will be occupied by the things and people you love instead of struggling to buy more things you don't need. Objects can't love you back – people can.

• The minimalist lifestyle inevitably brings peace. However, some people fear the future because they' 're afraid that if they don't have something, they won't be happy, they'll suffer, or they'll end up miserable. Minimalism is not poverty. It's just living a simple life. Money in the bank is always better than having no money and lots of possessions.

• Minimalism doesn't restrict having things. It just teaches you to shop more substantially. Spending less (or not at all) on unworthy items leaves you more money for things that'll bring value and positive change into your life.

When all benefits combine, the result is a happier, more fulfilled, and more meaningful life. To sum up, Minimalism's overall philosophy is in approaching your way of life and how you think about the physical things you own. Does the material attribute you hold in your life empower you to live out your dreams, or are they restricting your time and energy? Is the maintenance, organization, and storage of your items, giving you more time or less? Let the Minimalist philosophy inspire you in this journey of being more and having less.

The transformation of your current life to a minimalistic lifestyle can seem slightly daunting. This is because you're about to make a significant change in habits, consumption, finances, and your overall life. Though you know this difference is for the better, you're still scared of how it will all turn out.

Fear of the future and how your life will unfold is normal. You think you'll have less, when in fact, you'll have enough. If you've never experienced the minimalist lifestyle firsthand, this is probably your primary concern.

To build a minimalist life, first, you need to think like a minimalist. To do that, you're going to need to simplify your mindset, ambitions, emotions, and desires. Declutter your mind to make space for new, positive thoughts and empowering mindsets. You can then plan your minimalist home, room decor, food, work, etc.

Your mind creates your life. It establishes the "needs" and the "wants," and it leads you to achievement. I'm sure that during the reading of this book, you either thought or will think that you could never give up on some things. Because you're so emotionally attached to them, and you don't want to lose the beautiful memory that those objects remind you of.

There's a straightforward revelation behind this philosophy: memories are formed in your mind and stay in your heart forever. You decide to associate them with objects, and if the purpose is not present, you fear that the memory will fade away. However, fears, like limits, are often just an illusion. The reality is your mind is capable of keeping the memory alive for as long as you choose to. This is the exact reason why people tend to keep so much stuff – it's their treasure full of experiences they hold dear.

If you are still not convinced, we have a minimalist hack for you. If you have an item with no practical use but holds a treasured memory, try this: Take a picture of the thing, and you can look at it anytime you want without it taking up physical space.

So, if you think you could never give up on TV, your car, your too-many-bedroom home, your closet full of clothes and shoes, your favorite junk food, and more – think again. Your mind can adjust to and adopt anything – in this case, the minimalist lifestyle that will bring you many more positive changes than your current life does.

What follows are some simple steps, tips, and tricks to build a minimalist mindset:

- Recognize and select your needs. Often, people don't distinguish between what they need and what they want. This is true of material things. For example, we don't need a new appliance – we just want it because we think it'll make our life easier. We don't necessarily need 2-3 cars – we just want them for the same reason. The list goes on How much cabinet, pantry, and counter space all of your instruments occupy? Many machines are not used frequently enough to make life easier. Though a device may initially expedite a cooking task, count the amount of time it takes to clean and reassemble the apparatus after the function.

- Eliminate the "just-in-case" mentality. Much of the clutter in our apartments comes from hoarding items that we don't need immediately; rather, we think we might need them in some hypothetical future. We keep those items "just in case," fearing that we won't survive without them. Examples of 'just in case' items to eliminate are all those extra wicker baskets, various craft items. Another way to define 'just in case' items would be non-essential items (Examples: wicker baskets, various crafts, impractical shoes, or stacks of pens you keep). Contrast that with essential items such as fire extinguisher or first aid kits.

- Take your time. Becoming a minimalist is a massive change, and it doesn't happen overnight. Gradually, you'll start to realize how this lifestyle works, and adjusting your expectations should be by the process. It might happen in a couple of weeks; for some – a month or two and others, it might take longer. Have faith, keep your goals in mind, and everything will fall into place.

• Practice. The beginning may be hard, especially if you haven't tried minimalistic living before. The key toa successful transition is to practice. Start small. Get rid of things you haven't used in years (Especially three years or more); clean the garage; your pantry etc. With practice, you'll learn to select objects and classify them as essential or non-essential.

• Make a list of pros and cons. Be honest, objective, and view the question as if it wasn't your own. This

can significantly assist in the process.

• Being a new Mindful minimalist will take time and patience. Through this process, you will begin to value people more, objects less, and live life like never before. You will feel freer, as you only let go of all these non-essential items burdening you.

Why simple living is important

As humans, there are essential things we need to survive. We need clothes to keep us warm. We need food to nourish our bodies. We build homes for shelter.

And then there are things that he wasn't in life, for recreation and consumption.

Today, however, the majority of us want things that didn't exist before. These things could bring joy and satisfaction or unnecessary obsessiveness and addiction. The Internet has brought us unlimited information about the world around us. If you want immediate access to movies, you have Netflix. Instead of collecting music albums, you can download hundreds via iTunes. If you wanted to look smart, a digital bookshelf of literary classics could work its magic for you.

We can talk to people despite long distances. We can take our work anywhere. You can work on multiple things at once across several screens due to the onslaught of so many apps that could do anything. Life and work become more efficient, fast, and practical.

But progress has its pros and cons. We are bombarded by advertisements that reshape our desire for material possessions. We want bigger houses, faster cars, more advanced technology, fashionable clothes, expensive cuisine, and more.

Consumption is necessary, but in excess, it is not. Many of us work harder for things we may later realize we don't necessarily want. Owning too many things hampers not only our movements but also essential priorities. These prioritize a back seat until we understand later that we have lost so much time pursuing stuff we don't need.

And because of technological advances, we are expected to do more work since everything is almost automated. This leads to the habit of multitasking. It also doesn't help that the current addiction to screens drives most of us to have less sleeping hours, more stress, and unhealthy habits.

Do you feel like you are one of those people mentioned above? Are you working hard but feel like you are not accomplishing much? Do you realize that many of your possessions are stealing too much of your money, time, energy, and focus?

This can all be changed, but you have to change from thinking about decluttering your physical environment and mind. The first step to obtain this is to have more space to move around and help clear your head. You need to be in an environment where you are not always stressed out because you have too many things to do or don't have enough time to work on your goals and be with the people you love.

I believe you will recognize with me when I say that most of us desire to live comfortably and well-balanced lives. We all want space and enough time to reflect on how we want to spend each hour within a day and our future. This necessity for reflection is something that has been lacking in our modern life. We need to pull ourselves back to realize what is important to us.

And all this can be done by applying the concept of Minimalism.

Tips and tricks to minimalism

1. Write down your Reasons

The very first step to getting clear is knowing precisely what your reasons are for becoming a minimalist. You need to understand what is compelling you to make the change and why you are so dedicated. It is essential that you are completely clear about why you are making these changes and that the reasons are important to you. When we are passionate about our purpose, we are much more likely to succeed in what we set out to accomplish.

While you are getting clear on your reasons, take out a piece of paper and write them down. Some people may benefit from merely writing this down on a page in their journal, whereas others may want to take some time with it and turn their reasons into a piece of art that they can keep in a highly visible spot each day. What you choose to do will be up to you, but the most important thing is that you have your reasons readily available.

When you commence on a new journey in life, it can be easy to have mental "relapses," which will draw you back into a previous thinking way. You may fall back into old habits or patterns and think, "well, just this once!" But it's that exact mindset that leads you towards having a cluttered environment. During times like this, you want to go back to your written list of reasons and feel into them. Feel the emotion you put behind them and let it rise to the surface for you. The more you can genuinely feel those emotions, the easier it will be to remember why you are a minimalist and stay true to your desires.

2. Reclaim Your Time

So much time is wasted when you are trapped in a solely focused lifestyle on acquiring the latest and greatest. You spend several hours working, often at a job you don't even like. This generates stress, grief, anger, frustration, and other unwanted emotions that you must face regularly. Then, you must spend time maintaining all of the objects you have acquired. You need to organize them, reorganize them, clean them, service them, and otherwise preserve them. Then, you need to find the time to use them, which you likely rarely ever do spot, so you often end up acquiring objects that merely sit around for you to look at. If you travel or go anywhere, you likely bring more than is required just because you are too guilty to leave something behind knowing that you spent your precious money on it, which is a direct symbol for a time in your subconscious and potentially even in your conscious mind. Then, of course, you must invest time in acquiring more. So, you spend several hours in stores and malls getting frustrated over lineups, other shoppers, and anything else that may upset you. You may go into debt to acquire new things, or you may merely scrape from paycheck to paycheck because you don't want to stop purchasing new belongings. It can be a complicated trap to get stuck in.

Being a minimalist means that you get to reclaim your time. You get to stop working so hard to earn money to pay for items you don't have time to use, much less appropriately maintain. You get to stay spending hours a day working to pay off debt, cleaning, and staring at your house full of unused objects. You had the opportunity to thoroughly free yourself from all of the burdens that come along with these actions, both emotionally and physically. Ultimately, you get to reclaim your time to live a life that you want. You can do anything you want with the time you retrieve; the choice is entirely up to you.

In the beginning, it is a nice idea to take a page from your journal and write down all of the things you wish you had time for. What do you want to do that you haven't done because you don't have time? What are the things you have been putting off because there never seems to be a spare moment for you to complete them? How are you suffering in your own life because you don't give yourself enough time to enjoy it? This list is something you should refer to regularly. As you adopt the minimalist lifestyle, you will want to start checking things off of this list. If you ever feel unsure of what to do or where to go next, use this list as an opportunity to guide you. You can even build on the record as new ideas come up, regardless of how far or deep into your minimalist journey.

The most considerable part of being a minimalist is all of the free time you have. Many minimalists can even reduce their hours and go down to working part-time instead of full time because they only don't need all of the extra money, and they would rather spend time enjoying their life. Many even get to quit their job altogether and pursue a career that they are passionate about because they are no longer fearful of what will happen if they don't have a job to return to should anything go wrong. The freedom you gain from minimalism is unparalleled, and it is something you can look forward to enjoying your minimalist journey.

3. What Do You Value?

A significant part of the minimalist journey is learning about what you value most. When you are clear on what matters most to you, then you know exactly how to spend your time and resources on creating a life that you love, which is what minimalism is all about. You should spend some time getting to know what you value and becoming clear on it.

A great way to do this is to take your journal and start journaling. Write down what matters most to you and what you want to gain from life. What experiences make you feel productive with joy and happiness? What makes you thrilled to wake up and experience each new day as it comes? These are the things you want to enrich your life with. You should allow yourself to experience these as often as possible. When you are a minimalist, you have less to worry about taking care of your belongings and gaining more. Instead, you have the gift of more free time, which means that you get to spend your free time, however you want.

It is essential to know what your value is that it allows you to decide what you want to purchase and own in life. For example, if you appreciate the ability to hop in the car and go anywhere, you may want to keep your car, whereas if you don't mind taking public transit, it may be more beneficial if you get rid of your vehicle. The same goes for virtually anything else you may own.

4. Saying "No"

Learning to say "no" is essential, and it should be one of the first things you learn as a minimalist. You need to know how to say no to bringing more belongings into your house, how to say no to keep belongings in your home, and how to say no to doing things you don't want to do.

Many people believe minimalism is all about items, but it's not. It's about your time and your lifestyle as well. It is about eliminating anything that does not serve your highest good and learning to say no to anything that does not bring you joy. You want to learn how to say no and mean it, and never waiver in your answer. There is never a good enough purpose to do something that does not make you feel good overall.

Saying "no" can be hard at first, especially if you are not used to doing it. The more you practice, however, the easier it will be. You should learn to say no to smaller things first: shopping, bringing jobs home, joining e-mail newsletters, and other more accessible things. As you get used to it and it becomes easier for you, you can start saying it to

5. Minimalism is a Journey

Minimalism is a journey, not a lone goal. You will not wake up one morning with a trophy on your shelf because you 'accomplished' minimalism. Instead, minimalism is a lifestyle. You will be working towards your minimalist lifestyle for the rest of your life, or until you no longer desire to be a minimalist. But fear not, if you aren't already in love with it, most people find that they do become passionate about minimalism, and therefore it becomes easier to maintain the journey as they go on.

Any good lifestyle is a journey. As such, you can expect that your minimalism path will have ups and downs, the ins and outs, twists and turns, and all sorts of unexpected events. Nothing will go as planned, and in most instances, that is the beauty of life itself. These are just some of the things that you can look forward to enjoying during your minimalist journey.

Knowing that minimalism is a journey is very important. It means that you will not go into it thinking that you will master it or that it will all become more comfortable overnight. While it comprises many skills, it is not something that you can just learn and then walk away from. The balance required to maintain a minimalist lifestyle takes constant maintenance to ensure that you are not depriving yourself of your basic needs or overindulging in things that you do not need. You will always have to maintain this balance using tact, mindfulness, and practice. But, as with any pleasant journey, it is entirely worthwhile if you stay committed to the process.

Minimalism is a beautiful opportunity to learn about yourself and the things you love. You gain the ability to become the person you desire to be, and you can have any experience you want in life. The first part of mastering your mindfulness journey and your skills is to realize that you will never thoroughly learn them. Then, you need to get focused and find ways to stay focused on your journey's purpose. Once you have, you will be ready to have any experience you desire in life. The money, time, and resources will be available to you because you have gotten your priorities straight.

6. Store Things Out of Sight

Many people feel compelled to store things on the counter or in a space where they can grab it and then toss it back down. While this might be convenient for grabbing it partly, it can also be inconvenient for the rest. After all, rolling things back down often leads to messing, and the mess is likely what lead you to minimalism to begin with. The first thing you need to do is learn to store items properly.

Ideally, you want to store things out of sight. In drawers, cabinets, cupboards, and closets are a great place to keep items that you aren't using every single day. This means that you do not have to look at it, aside from when you want actually to use it. Ensuring that you are still keeping them organized and under control when you are organizing things back into these out-of-sight places is absolutely key. You do not want to have them cluttering up your out-of-sight areas, as this will merely lead to more stress. Instead, put them away in an organized and logical fashion. This keeps everything out of sight so that your physical surroundings are cleaner, and it remains everything easy to access and use.

7. Reduce Cooking Time

Many people dislike cooking for lengthy periods of time. If you love cooking and don't mind cooking regularly, then this doesn't apply to you! However, if you dislike cooking and often find yourself eating "convenience" items costly and take up space, it might be time to learn how to cook without spending so much time doing so!

Meal prepping is a tremendous way to get a bunch of cooking out of the way so that you don't have to worry about cooking so much regularly. You can prepare meals for a few days at a time so that all you have to do is heat them and eat them! Another great idea is the ingredient prepping. This means that you pre-peel, cut, chop, slice, dice, cube, and store items in a way that makes them easy to cook with. When it comes time to prepare, you merely grab enough to melt with and begin the cooking process!

8. Delegate

Not everything has to be done by you. It may feel like you have to do everything alone, but the reality is that you do not. You can easily delegate tasks elsewhere so that you have more time to focus on you and what you want to and need to get done. If you have a family living with you, this is easy. Only create a chore-list, and everyone has the unique tasks that they are expected to get done to keep the house operating functionally on a daily, weekly, and monthly basis.

If you live alone, on the other hand, it may be a bit harder to delegate. However, there are still tasks that you can transfer out. For example, if you hate grocery shopping, you can order groceries right to your door. There are many services available that offer local-delivery of fresh ingredients. In fact, you can even find services that will deliver locally-sourced organic items that are healthy and convenient. You can delegate other tasks as well, depending on what you are looking to charge. Some people even hire maids or housekeepers with all of their spare money to keep them from doing any of the extra work around the house!

9. Take Breaks

Taking regular technology breaks is essential. As a society, we spend an enormous amount of time attached to devices. Our screen time racks up fast, and we often don't even realize it's happening. Between all of our unique tools, it can be easy to lose time in the online space. A great way to reclaim your time is to take regular tech breaks.

Tech breaks mean that you put away all unnecessary technology for a period. You might do daily tech breaks for a few hours per day, 24 hours break once per week, or even longer breaks. Exactly how long you choose to take tech breaks and how often is up to you, but it is recommended that you take them frequently. This allows you to recall how to experience joy in life without relying on the instant gratification of technology that often does not serve our highest good.

When it comes to taking tech breaks, you want to eliminate computers, tablets, cell phones, smartwatches, televisions, and gaming devices. Stuff you need for cooking, fobs to enter your house or your car, and other such technology devices are perfectly acceptable to continue using. The benefit comes from reducing and eliminating screen time regularly so that you can stay focused on life itself and all that life has to offer. These breaks are excellent at helping you eliminate technology addictions and reclaim your time.

10. Clean Up Social Media

We often spend a great deal of time on social media. A good idea is actually to clean up your social media. Regularly, you should unfollow pages and groups you don't like, eliminate friends you do not enjoy having around, and clean up your pages so that they are more favorable to you.

Spending a significant amount of time-consuming information on social media means that you are exposing yourself to a volatile environment. However, you do have a degree of control over what you see and who you see online, which means that you have the opportunity to make it a more favorable environment for yourself. You should regularly take time to clean up your social media accounts to remain as positive as possible. That way, any time you spend on your social media accounts will be positive and practical.

11. Morning Routines

There are many pieces of information floating around about what makes an effective morning routine, but something to consider is what doesn't make a solid morning routine. Ineffective morning routines are virtually any routine that has too many things going on. In the morning, you likely have two goals: wake up in a positive mood and acquire enough energy to tackle the day ahead of you. Every single activity you do in the morning should fulfill these needs. If you find you are partaking in any morning routine activities that are not beneficial to you, you should remove these events from your routine. It is not always necessary to substitute them with anything else; you merely need to create a morning routine that serves you.

You will often read that a routine should be an absolute length or include some aspects to be productive. The reality is that you can have a productive 10-minute morning routine, or you can have a productive 45 minute or more extended morning routine. The amount of time you use to carry out your schedule and what is actually involved is special to you and can only consist of items that make you feel energized and optimistic in your day. If it just takes you five minutes to do that, great! If it makes you an hour to do this, that's completely fine as thoroughly.

12. *Other Routines*

There are many different routines you partake in throughout your day, as well. In many instances, we establish a method and never revisit it to see if we are using the most efficient manner available to us. It is a good idea to visit routine tasks you do regularly to make them more efficient and effective, if possible.

For example, perhaps you always take the same way to work, but due to the installation of new traffic measures, a new route would be quicker or easier for you to choose. However, perhaps because you never revisit your routine, you are still making the long way to work. Now would be an excellent time to begin with, this method and change it. Alternatively, perhaps you always do the dishes by washing and thoroughly drying and then rewashing them. In reality, you can directly learn to stack them more efficiently, not to have to wipe them in between. In this case, you can only stack them better, or wash them more frequently, and make the task significantly more comfortable.

It is a good idea to take a look at anything you do daily without thinking about it and find any ways you might be able to enhance these routines to become more efficient and efficient. The better these methods serve you, the more relaxed you will be able to get through them and spend the rest of your free time enjoying life.

Your time is valuable, and a significant part of minimalism is recognizing the value in your time and spending it wisely. Many people place an enormous amount of money and material objects and fail to realize how negatively this affects their time, which tends to be more valuable than money or substantial items. Minimalism is all about learning to replace your value on time and spend it in a way that serves you. You want to spend your time effectively and efficiently so that you can gain the most enjoyment and positivity out of life possible.

13. Forget About Perfection

Something vital for you to learn is that you need to forget about perfection. Perfection adds stress to our lives and makes it harder for us to enjoy life itself. We spend so much time trying to get everything right that we fail to spend time doing. Applying minimalist skills to your life means that you eliminate the need to be perfect and learn how to be. Of course, it doesn't say that you don't need to give it you're all. Instead, it means that you just give it your best, and then you appreciate it.

Forgetting about perfection and focusing on doing means that you accomplish more in your life. When you let go of your attachment towards doing things entirely, you give yourself the freedom to feel more confident and happy with what you do accomplish when you try your best. You take away the constant feelings of inadequacy and incompetence, and you allow yourself to feel powerful and confident.

14. Do What You Love

You should practice investing time in doing something you love every single day. Waiting to enjoy time doing what you love is never beneficial, and it can reduce your quality of life. Doing something you like every single day allows you to enjoy your life every single day, as well. You don't have to do something major, but you should do at least one thing per day to help you enjoy life more.

Some ideas of what you might do include:

Cooking or eating a meal that you love.

Going on a scenic walk somewhere you like.

Practicing a hobby or activity that you enjoy.

Doing any other number of smaller things you want.

You might also do something more significant, such as travel somewhere, take a new class, or do something more involved that you would want to do. There's no ceiling on what you can or can't do while you do what you love. Only do it.

Also, you should learn to turn everything into something you enjoy more. You may not necessarily love everything, but you can certainly make it more enjoyable for you. For example, instead of cleaning the dishes, see if you can turn it into a game and make it more enjoyable. Or, instead of only sweeping the floors, set the broom into your make-shift microphone and have an at-home concert for one. There are so many opportunities to transform day-to-day tasks into those you enjoy creatively; there is no reason to spend each day doing mundane things out of obligation.

15. Evaluate Your Schedule

Take some time to think about your schedule. Do you enjoy everything that is on it? Is it fulfilling you or making you feel happy? If you are not satisfied with your program, you need to adjust it to fit your needs. If it is overwhelming, find a way to tone it down and make more time for relaxation and peace. If your schedule is underwhelming, find some new activities that you can add to your regular schedule. Sometimes you may not have an overwhelming or underwhelming plan, but rather very little of what's on, it lights you up and makes you feel happy. If this is the case, you should find a way to add more to it to bring you joy and make you love your life even more.

Your schedule can be a fantastic tool to help you experience more joy, or it can be a dangerous device that destroys your happiness. If you can manage your schedule wisely, you can have an incredible selection of plans set up that allow you to control your responsibilities and enjoy life itself. Ideally, you want to learn how you can balance your schedule in this harmonious way.

16. *Explore the World*

Exploring the world is a valuable means to add happiness, joy, and education into your daily life. Of course, most of us can't pack up and explore the world every single day or at the drop of a hat. However, living a more minimalistic lifestyle means that you have much more freedom to explore your way. With fewer expenses and more time, you can do whatever you want for the most part. You should take advantage of this by exploring the world.

You can explore the world around you or travel out and explore elsewhere in the world. There is no limit or rules on what you can or should do when you are investigating. Directly go where your heart takes you. Each new exploration will bring you so much value and knowledge in your life, and most will bring about a broad sense of joy and happiness that enrich your life in ways that other learning resources only cannot.

The world is a brilliant place, and one of the joys of being a minimalist is that it becomes easier for you to explore and enjoy the world. Whether you are hiking, camping, flying, traveling by train, going across countries, or staying in your backyard, nothing beats exploring the world around you and getting to know it better.

17. Do Something New

Have you ever felt like time just melts away? One moment it's a blistering hot summer day, and you're sipping an iced drink, and the next moment it's a cold winter day three years later, and you're in the same spot, only drinking a hot beverage? Research suggests that time melts away because we are continually doing the same thing every day. Average individuals wake up, go to work, spend eight hours working, come home, relax, go to bed, and then do it all over again.

As a minimalist, you have the perfect opportunity to break this cycle and lead a life where every day is precious and diverse from the last. Each one is memorable and serves a purpose in allowing you to be a happier version of yourself. All you have to do is practice doing something new each day. Or at the very least, something new each week. You can do something as small as making an original recipe or driving a new route or something more substantial, like traveling to a new place or picking up a new hobby. Doing something new breaks up the mundane and puts some pep back into your routine. It makes each day stand out and unique from the last and from the rest that is yet to come. It makes life exciting and keeps sparks. Time will slow down a little as each day won't melt into one another, making life difficult for you to enjoy overall. It is indeed an excellent opportunity to retake control over your life and start living one you love to the fullest.

18. Release Ties

How many times are you holding onto because you are too scared to let go? Or because giving go would be too inconvenient. These relations may be to friends, objects, places, or any other number of things that you hold onto in life. Relationships are common, and you will never get rid of your tendency to create relations towards stuff in your life. However, you must regularly weed your life and rid yourself of the relationship that does not serve you or bring you joy in life.

Releasing ties allows you to let go of the past and open yourself up to bigger and better things. You are granted the chance to refresh yourself and open up space in your life. You stop feeling guilty or even ashamed around specific people, places, or things, and you start feeling free once again.

It can be hard to release ties, primarily when we have invested a significant amount of time, emotion, or energy into keeping them. However, the value you can gain from freeing yourself from those ties is immeasurable. Think about how much more devastated you will be if you invest even more time, emotion, and energy into something that will serve you. Eventually, it will filter out, either because it naturally ends or because you just can't take any more. It is better to cut ties when you are in control and have the power to do so independently.

19. Fall in Love with Yourself

You are the only person you have to live with every single day of your life. Others will come and go. Some will be there for a long time, but none will ever be immediately by your side for every day of every minute of your life. Only you will be. If you don't take the time to fall in love with yourself and create a relationship with yourself that you love, you don't have much fun in life.

Falling in love with yourself is essential, and you should invest in it every day. Think of it as a marriage: if you don't spend the time to work on it, it will fall apart. Of course, there will be ups and downs, but you should always take the time to be gentle with yourself and love yourself as you would your spouse. Only enjoy yourself even more. You are valued, and you are worth it, and as a result, you should always find the time to fall in love with yourself daily. You deserve it.

20. Evaluate Your In-Home Entertainment

How much time do you spend entertaining in your home? For many of us, we don't consider on a daily or even a weekly basis. If this is true for you, you need to sort through your stuff and eliminate what you don't need. There is no need to hold on to things for entertaining guests if you rarely have guests over. This only requires you to use up storage space for something you don't need, which goes against minimalism's fundamental values. It is time for you to get honest with yourself about your entertainment schedule and reduce your entertaining items to reflect that program.

Your daily life can be significantly affected by minimalism. We frequently find ourselves living an everyday life that is uncomfortable, unfulfilling, and often filled with unnecessary activities. If you want to change your life, you need to embrace minimalist values beyond just your physical belongings. You need to be willing to apply them elsewhere in life, too, so that you can free yourself from all that does not serve you or bring you joy and lead a life that does.

Chapter 6: Taking Control of What You Do

Some people are aware of the connections between their anxious thoughts and the feelings and behavior that associate those thoughts. For example, Mark understands that when he has to attend a meeting at work, he's likely to become stressed and worried a couple of days leading to the meeting, and he always suffers from a small migraine.

Others know when they are thinking anxious thoughts. Still, any physical symptoms they go through-headaches, digestive problems, and tension within their shoulders are considered something quite different and don't associate them with being anxious. If they reveal a physical symptom, they believe it means they have different physical problems. And that can just increase their fears and worries.

Others may only be aware of the physical symptoms and not even realize they have been anxious about something.

It's important to note that anxiety has behavioral and physical features and cognitive elements, and each feature can activate another. Your thoughts can trigger physical feelings. If you were to take a thin slice of lemon, for instance, your mouth would likely begin watering. If you see someone yawning, you may find yourself yawning too.

Similarly, anxiety isn't all planted in your head. Anxiety happens throughout your body too. So, part of dealing with anxiety requires that you manage the physical elements in constructive ways. In fact, you might discover that, for many circumstances, changing what you do may be easier or more practical than changing how and what you believe. And once you control the physical feelings, the thoughts calm down and become more rational and reasonable.

All of us have experienced physical feelings that accompany anxiety: feeling hot and cold, increased heartbeat, butterflies in the stomach, feeling faint, trembling, and so forth. There are many different methods in which people experience physical anxiety, but they are all connected to our "fight or flight" response.

How Worry and Anxiety Affects the Body

When a difficulty, problem, or challenge avails itself, your body gets ready to deal with it. The fight or flight feedback causes your body's nervous system to produce hormones like cortisol and adrenaline. These hormones can increase blood sugar levels, which the body can use immediately for fuel to defend itself against a dangerous situation.

However, when you're worried, if you think things like, "I'll get horribly lost" or "What if I commit a mistake on this project?"

You will be creating fear with your thoughts of danger and disaster, and your body responds by triggering the symptoms related to fear and stress.

Once excessive fuel within the blood isn't used for physical activities, the hormones increase, heartbeat increases, muscle tension, and shallow breathing result in more long-term symptoms like:

Headaches

Digestive problems

Irritability and inability to focus

Fatigue and tiredness

Nervous energy

Clenched jaw

If you constantly suffer from these symptoms, it's crucial to see a doctor rule out unrelated physical challenges. And in case the physical symptoms do happen because of anxiety, there is, of course, medication present to take control of physical effects.

The most common medications for long-term treatment of anxiety are antidepressants, which restore the brain's balance of chemicals.

Anxiety attacks may also be controlled with rapid-acting medications such as diazepam, important for short-term treatment of dangerous panic attacks.

Anxiety and its physical side effects may be controlled with beta-blockers, which are normally used to handle heart conditions and high blood pressure. Beta-blockers such as propranolol reduce the heart rate and relax blood vessels, which can relieve physical symptoms.

You might attempt to control the symptom that disturbs you the most yourself. For instance, if you experience stress in your digestion because of anxiety, you may consume over-the-counter stomach medication. However, if you suffer from headaches, you might consume painkillers from the chemist, and so forth.

They may or may not assist. Although there are other things, you should do little to regulate the physical symptoms of fear.

Acknowledge and Accept

Start by becoming aware that you are experiencing a physical symptom of anxiety. Experience and pay attention to it without focusing on it or reacting to it like an emergency. Apply a mindful technique and accept that whatever the reason you do believe you do.

Reduce Physical Feelings

Once you acknowledge and accept the physical sensations you experience, you can bring down the physical feelings.

Your means of breathing has a direct impact on your physical symptoms. Whenever you're in danger, going through an emergency, rather than breathing at a normal rate, you begin to breathe quickly and shallowly from your upper lungs, breathing in more air than your body requires.

If you fail to respond to the possible danger with fight or flight, then you might experience the uncomfortable symptoms that occur with anxiety, panic: feeling light-headed, confusion, dizziness, numbness in the hands or feet, the feelings of nausea.

The good news is that by altering your breathing, you can change the above symptoms. By taking charge of your breathing, the following takes place:

Your blood pressure decreases.

You start to feel more at ease and calm.

Your demand for oxygen decreases. Your muscle tension weakens.

It's important to understand that there's a slight difference between calming back down and getting het up. The distinction lies in the timing. The emergency reaction is immediate. All those physical changes occur together immediately.

It takes longer, however, for your body to "calm down." While it takes longer for the body to respond to a calming response, you can trigger it to happen.

It can actually allow you to calm down the physical feelings if you can master how to control your breathing. It might be advice you've heard before, but it really can help.

Master a natural breathing method that provides you enough oxygen and regulates the release of carbon dioxide.

Focusing on your breathing achieves two things: calms everything down-your quick heartbeat and your racing thoughts. It can reduce or distract your mind and provide it something valuable to reflect. It's mindful; when you concentrate on your breathing, you are focusing on something that is taking place now. It helps to ground you.

Of course, you might discover thoughts popping up as you breathe. Just let them come and go and redirect your focus to your breathing.

Regulating your breathing also has the advantage of being a simple thing you can do anywhere, any time. You can do it any time you want. Remind yourself by putting a sticky note with the words 'breathe' and stick it on your computer.

There are different ways you can control your breathing.

Here are some of the methods

1. Feel your breathing

First, place one hand on your chest and feel your breath rushing into and out of your body. Discover the natural rhythm. Understand the coolness of the air as you breathe in and the warmth of the air as you exhale.

2. Count your breathing

Breathe and count forward and backward. Start by counting up to 7 as you inhale, and then back down from 7 as you exhale, then count to 6 as you inhale, and back from 6 as you exhale. Keep counting until you get to 3 and then return to counting up to 7. As you attain the lower numbers, count more slowly.

3. Reflect on your breathing

Apply your imagination. Breathe in as if you're accepting the scent of a flower. Exhale like you're blowing bubbles. Assume that your breathes are like the ocean waves. They come and go. Or imagine breathing out to the limits of the universe and inhale from there into your body. Or you can inhale color; assume the color of the air occupying your lungs but your whole body.

When you control breathing, you will also manage your thoughts and behavior—the cognitive and features of worry and anxiety.

Trust Your Body's Ability to Breathe

What if it's breathing that's causing you problems?

When you feel anxious, you might experience a slight tension in your throat or chest. It's your chest and throat muscles that are tense, but the feeling can cause you to believe that you're not receiving sufficient air. This can then result in panic and light-headedness, feeling like you have insufficient oxygen or that you might stop breathing together.

Before you realize it, a cycle of anxiety starts as one fear triggers the other. What to do?

While it might feel like it, you are not really going to stop breathing. You can confirm this to yourself by taking a deep breath and holding it for as long as possible. Once you hold your breath for however long, your body will attain a state where it automatically causes you to breathe in quickly. As usual, your breathing will, at a certain point, return to normal. Remember that!

Performing this exercise can allow you to feel confident in your body's ability to breathe. You will understand that whatever you do with your breathing, your body is normally in control and always monitors your breathing for you.

But, if you realize that focusing on your breathing just worsens things-that once you're anxious, whatever you set your mind on becomes a problem. Then, it is good not to think about your breathing at all. Understand and try to accept it. If you think that your breathing is too rapid and shallow, then let it be shallow and rapid.

Instead, you may want to attempt something unique.

Stand up and Get Moving: Exercise and Physical Activity

Keep in mind, when you're feeling anxious or fearful, your body produces stress hormones, like cortisol and adrenaline. These increase physical symptoms that you experience, such as a racing pulse. If there is nothing you can do about the cause of your worry, then the same hormones can prevent you from becoming angry for some time.

Choosing to do a physical activity can help.

Physical activity consumes adrenaline, reduces tension, and can prevent you from those worrying thoughts. Probably, playing football, running, and other fitness exercises can help. But it doesn't have to be a coordinated sports event or structured exercise program.

Any physical exercise such as washing your car, gardening, or walking briskly around the block can help.

As well as reducing tension and consuming adrenaline, physical exercise is a great way to help prevent worries from eating you up because it can divert the focus from your brain to your body.

Of course, when you're feeling anxious, physical exercise can appear like the last thing you want to do. However, once you get moving, you may find it can create a difference, relieving anxiety symptoms, and ensuring you feel better.

If you enjoy being outdoors, walk, run, cycle, or throw the dog ball. Running, cycling, and swimming help you to remain active at your own pace, and you can do them alone. However, you may want to request a friend to join you might like the company.

Be active in your way. Perform it at your own speed and ability. What can you do? Imagine two or three physical exercises that you like or you can do. You will be more likely to perform them when you need to release your anxious energy.

As well as consuming the adrenaline and other hormones and letting muscles relax, physical activity and exercise can produce feel-good brain chemicals.

Walking is fine. Anyone can do it at any age and fitness level. It's right for your heart, your head, and your wallet. Walking is also a perfect way to link with nature. Research indicates that walking in green places reduces stress levels, boosts mood, and improves psychological well-being and concentration.

You can walk on your or with other people, and it will not cost a thing.

If you are unable to get outside, look for a YouTube film that you can follow. Or perform some housework like make the bed.

Whatever you do, it will also be a distraction that can get you away from the cycle of negative thoughts that increase anxiety.

The Food You Consume

If you're anxious, how and what you eat determines how you and your stomach feel.

Fried, fatty, and rich sauces can cause you to feel queasy. Coffee, alcohol, and high sugar content foods can make you feel wired. Not consuming these foods is unlikely to cure anxiety, but it will help.

If you experience irritable bowel changes, controlling your diet will treat your symptoms.

But, there is no specific diet for persons with the condition. What works well for you will depend on your symptoms and how you respond to various foods when you're anxious.

Whatever your symptoms, it might help to:

Take your time when eating.

Have daily meals.

Limit the amount of coffee, tea, and fizzy drinks you take.

Lastly, when anxiety creeps into your stomach, try some of the breathing methods. They can help reduce the symptoms of a disturbing stomach.

Ways to Cultivate a Mental Attitude That Will Generate Peace and Happiness

The same way everyone has different thoughts and physical feelings when anxious, each of us behaves differently.

If you were feeling anxious because you were waiting for an email, phone call, or letter to tell you whether or not you would be provided with the job, you might walk up and down the room. Another person might sit and bite their nails. Someone else might smoke. Someone else might decide to perform their rituals.'

We each behave when we are worried about different things, including what has caused the anxiety, our ability to control the situation, and how the circumstance is similar to our past experiences.

Probably you avoid circumstances that make you feel anxious in the past, and you also avoid similar events and situations that you think will make you more anxious.

Avoiding behaviors can involve 'doing' or not doing' things. 'Doing' behaviors might be ritualistic and compulsive behaviors like excessively washing hands, counting, or checking. They might entail dependency tendencies: depending on, for instance, other people, medication to allow you to avoid anxious feelings and thoughts.

When total avoidance is impossible, you may decide to escape behaviors: leaving or escaping in the middle of a situation. For instance, if you could not avoid or get out of a social situation, you might discover a means to leave as soon as you can.

One of the issues with avoidance behaviors is that they place you in a fearful state. For instance, suppose you avoid a social situation at the last minute because of your anxious thoughts. You step at the door, and your anxiety increases. You turn back and return home.

Once you arrive home, your physical feelings decrease: your breathing rate goes back to normal, your temperature returns to normal, your heart rate starts to reduce. This means your body reinforces your avoidance. Your body relaxes and notifies you that you took the correct action.

You experience a sense of comfort and relief as you say to yourself, "Thank God I didn't step in. Suppose I had? My heart would have beat fast so hard that I would have experienced a panic attack."

The decrease in your physical symptoms, plus your thoughts about what would have taken place if you had gone to the party, will boost your decision to avoid similar social circumstances in the future.

Well, ask yourself: how much of your mental energy and time has avoidance coping consumed you? How has it destroyed your relationships with colleagues, friends, and family? How has it impacted your self-esteem and confidence?

Avoidance behaviors are just a crutch-they offer temporary and inappropriate relief. The challenge is, avoidance behaviors make you think that you've successfully solved the problem of whatever is causing your anxiety.

Although avoidance may make you feel better in the short term, you never get the opportunity to discover how to deal with your fears and take charge of situations. It either doesn't happen to you that there must be a better way to respond or if it does, you don't know how to resolve what is making you anxious. But confronting your fears is the main thing. You can achieve this using an approach known as 'solution-focused problem-solving.' It entails concentrating on what you can alter instead of features of the circumstances that are beyond your limit. You spent your time and energy dealing with solutions and not the problems.

Solution-Focused Technique

This requires that you start by accepting your anxious thoughts and feelings.

Realizing and accepting your symptoms will act as the key to the next steps. When you are experiencing problems using new skills, consider whether you are using the principle of acceptance.

If you can accept your anxious thoughts and feelings, you offer your rational side of the mind the chance to start working for you.

It's important to recall that when you're anxious, the highly reactive side of your brain takes over, and the thinking side of your brain shuts down.

Rather than allow initial anxiety to trigger you to identify a constructive solution to whatever you're worried about when you're worried, you've let those worries grow and overwhelm your mind.

The first step is to reduce the anxiety-provoking amygdala within your brain and involve the neocortex: the thinking side of your brain. It requires effort, commitment, and practice, but you can do this.

You can still engage the thinking side of your brain by offering it something simple and neutral to consider. It can be recalling what you had to consume for each meal yesterday. Or you can try to count backward from 50 or recite an alphabet backward. It might involve responding to a few clues in a crossword puzzle.

Don't make it so difficult a hard task that you give up and allow your mind to return to your worries.

Once you feel like you're able to think straight, you can start to deal with whatever it is worrying you and generating anxiety.

Learn to Plan Rather Than Worry

There's no question that worrying can be useful when it triggers you to take action and solve a problem. But feeling anxious doesn't change a situation. Switching into a cycle of worry and anxiety will not allow you to think clearly or allow you to address a potential problem.

You must take action: helpful action. Deal with the problem, create changes, and see some progress. Then you would feel in control and less anxious. You will have shifted from causing problems to finding solutions.

If you can adopt a beginner's mind on something you have been worried about before, you have a high chance of making it different from last time.

While this can sound like counter-intuitive advice, it can help you begin to identify and accept what the worst-case scenario would be. The reason is that once you have accepted what it is you fear taking place, then you know what it is that you're up against. You can proceed to what your options are to reduce or handle the worst-case scenario.

For instance, if you were scared about driving somewhere new, your worst-case scenario might be that you would get lost, drive in circles and probably run out of petrol.

A worst-case scenario with an incoming deadline is that you won't hit the deadline, your manager will get angry,

and everyone else will assume you're incompetent.

Or, in a different case, you could be headed to a party where you don't know anyone. The worst-case scenario is that you end up in a situation with no one to talk to and experience a panic attack.

What are you scared about currently? What is the worst that might happen?

Whatever it is, you can learn to be organized rather than worry. Worry consumes your mind. On the other hand, a plan provides you with a positive focus.

There are six steps you can take:

1.   Highlight the specific problem and the worst-case scenario.

2. Highlight the best-case scenario.

3. Identify possible solutions and options.

4. Determine the options or solutions.

5. Divide your solution into manageable steps'

6. Review the result.

Highlight the Specific Problem and the Worst-Case Scenario

Well, the first thing to ask yourself is, what is the worst that might happen?

Write your response down. Try to be as specific as possible.

Determine the Best-Case Scenario

Next, highlight what you would really want to happen. What is the best-case scenario would be? This is an approach to determining your values and finding out what will help you.

Reflect on what you would like the result to be. For instance, would you like the result to be that you can achieve it with the looming deadline? Or would you like the deadline to be extended, and you have enough time?

When you feel anxious, you can lose sight of what it is you want. You're too busy thinking about what you don't want.

Understanding what you want and where you want to reach makes a successful result possible.

Determine Options and Possible Solutions

Once you decide what you would like to happen, think of what you can do that might help you realize the best-case scenario.

Don't feel like you need to identify a perfect solution. Just determine what you can change instead of elements of the situation that are beyond your control.'

With a work deadline, for instance, the options might include:

Request someone to help you

Work overtime to have it finished on time

Determine what the major parts are that require timely completion and which parts can be handed in later.

Discuss with your manager for additional time.

The point here is to come up with possibilities. It might be necessary to consider.

What, if anything, you had done before in the same situation that was not relevant?

Something that you have done in the same situation that was useful.

The kind of ideas and solutions your friends or family would suggest.

All these represent ideas. This process of looking for options will extend you past your normal method of thinking and behavior.

Make sure you write your options, ideas, and solutions down so that you can see them. Writing things down can be helpful for several reasons. First, by writing them down, it forces you to define your options more clearly. Secondly, instead of retaining them in your head, writing your options and ideas down breaks down your ideas.

Change your mind to positive possibilities and tell yourself that you can make it different from last time. This is why teaching your brain to think positively is so important. It will simplify your process of searching for positive alternatives when you're looking for new options.

Select One of the Options or Solutions

Once you have listed down a few options, select a solution from the options you have highlighted. Which solutions or actions feel right to you? Would it be unavoidable to go through the reasons 'for' and 'against' each idea?

If you are still doubting, don't include your worries by attempting to determine the right solution. Overthinking can result in confusion and damage to you so that you end up with no-decision.

When the situation supports it, stepping away for some time can help you see things with fresh eyes and a new mind when you come back to it.

Don't wait, though, until you are completely sure about something before you take action. The sooner you achieve something, the better you will feel confident, control, and less worried.

Just remember that you might never understand for sure the result of a given action, but you can always be ready to overcome possible challenges that arise.

Divide Your Solution Into Manageable Steps

To simplify things, you will need to divide your selected solution into smaller steps. The number of steps needed will vary based on the situation.

Therefore, if you were worried about going to a party that you will not know anyone, you don't know what you will say, or you feel stupid. The worst-case scenario will be that you experience a panic attack. The best-case scenario is that you will feel reasonably calm, speak to a few people, and then return home feeling good about it all.

Developing steps translate into a plan. Once you have a plan with positive, manageable steps, combined with positive thoughts about the event, breathing techniques, acceptance of your anxious feelings, etc. You are more likely to control.

If you find yourself apprehensive again at some moment, note, 'Stop! I've got a proposal! 'Tell yourself about the actions you are taking to keep your mind on that.

What things would you often avoid because they make you feel anxious? Start small. Start with things that would not be difficult. It doesn't matter whether they are minimal steps; the purpose is to allow you to regain sufficient control to feel that, little by little, you can regain enough control to feel that. Even the smallest behaviors are steps in the right direction.

Visualize a positive result. Create images for yourself where you see yourself achieving successful results. Rather than think about the worst scenario in your mind, you play out the best.

The more you visualize yourself coping and coming out on the other side, the more likely it will take place. Keep in mind, seeing yourself coping ensures that your brain believes that it is, indeed, possible.

Review the Result

Once you've gone through the situation, review the result. What worked? What went well? What allowed it to go well? If it didn't go as planned, what did you learn?

More Ways to Cultivate a Mental Attitude That Will Generate Peace and Happiness

You can apply different approaches in your life, and here are several ways to do so.

1. Occupy your mind with thoughts of courage, health, peace, and hope

Your dominant thought will establish reality. If you keep complaining about not having enough, those "not enough" feelings will start pouring in.

2. Don't try to get even without enemies, because if we hurt ourselves far more than we hurt them. Don't waste a minute reflecting on people you don't like.

This is very critical. Forgive! Don't be one of those people who wait for karma to take a toll.

3. Count your blessings, not your problems 4. Don't imitate others. Discover yourself and be yourself, for "envy is ignorance" and "imitation is suicide."

5.   When fate sends us a lemon, try and create lemonade.

6. Don't forget your unhappiness by trying to establish a little happiness for others. When you do good to others, you are best to yourself.

7.   Remember that the only way to discover happiness is not to expect gratitude but to provide for the joy of giving.

How to Calm Worries, Anxiety, and Emotional Stress

Talking to someone, like a friend or family member, about emotional stress, anxiety, and other effects it's causing on you can help you in various ways. It might make them decide to help you know how much you feel and what you go through. They may have gone through similar feelings and can share their experiences.

Raising your worries can snatch your scariness. Usually, just having someone to listen to you because they care can help.

If you cannot talk to a partner, friend, or family member or do and are not helpful or feel the desire to talk things over with someone who is not directly involved like a doctor or counselor.

Positive Individuals

The way people respond to you can set a difference in how you feel about yourself-to, your self-esteem, confidence, and your ability to regulate anxious feelings and thoughts. You need positive people in your life.

Be creative in your thinking. The positive people you choose do not necessarily have to be close family or people you know. Maybe the person you can turn to in times of trouble is your GP. Probably someone on TV could be the person who makes you laugh. The person who motivates you could be an individual you have read about who has defeated adversity.

You might have a different person or several individuals for each circumstance or the same individual. While having one optimistic person in your life can make all the difference to your potential to control these situations, try and look for a few people who, in their different ways, might be your support network.

For every positive individual out there, though, there is perhaps one negative individual. Others can be considered as "drains or radiators." Radiators refer to those who can take away your energy and resources. Their negativity can boost your anxiety; just the feeling of being around them can make you feel worried and anxious. They might, for instance, remain critical of you or just be critical of everyone. They make fun of your anxiety or emotional stress and tell you you're ridiculous.

On the flip side, radiators are likely to respond to you positively. We all require 'radiators" in our lives; just being around radiators can be reassuring.

Of course, it's not always practical to eliminate negative people from your life. However, the best you can do is spend less time around negative people and more time with positive people.

Keeping distance from negative individuals involves reading about other people who are considered victims. The highlight is on their situation's unfairness and suffering, and problems never appear to be resolved. Distance yourself from stories that condemn and make fun of magazines and websites. Instead, search for stories about people who motivate you.

Read about famous individuals who have dealt with difficult times in their lives. What do you think that helped them cope? Their stories can motivate you and allow you to think along positive lines.

Help Other People

When you're emotionally distressed, worried, and anxious, it's easy to feel overwhelmed with your own troubles. But if you look beyond yourself and discover other people going through the same, you may realize that your worries take a back seat. Help others, and in the process, you help yourself; you create a fresh perspective on your own life and situations.

Develop the confidence to think of others and to do something for them.

Studies demonstrate that even assisting one person can generate feelings and attitudes, resulting in better physical health, overall happiness, and mental health.

Helping others generates a positive mindset. And this is because you need to actively identify positive methods to reach out to help and support a person suffering or finding it hard to cope. It pushes you into a cycle of positive thinking and behavior.

Kind gestures allow you to focus on yourself and allow you to reach out to someone else. You might want to identify your own system of helping other people, assist a neighbor in need by getting some shopping once a week, or volunteer to cut their grass.

If you know a person in need of a volunteer, offer your service to them. Just ask how you could help make a situation favorable. You may feel you have too little to offer, but whether it's a cup of tea, an invite to dinner, or an offer to help carry something, it's thinking and being ready to do something for others that's important.

Reach out to people you haven't spoken to in a while. Do it today. Send them an email or card to allow them to know you were thinking about them. Find out how they are. Find out what's happening in their life, even if it's to request how their children, job, or health care. By just reflecting on what you can think about diverts the focus from yourself.

If you need support and company when you help others, you can volunteer your time and assist with a local community group.

There's a lot of things you can do. As a volunteer, you can make a critical contribution to various aspects of community life.

Try to search for an activity that provides:

A chance to apply the skills you already have or one that offers training to learn new skills.

The chance for constant help: A few hours a week. The frequency of assistance is important because it's a regular opportunity to eliminate worries.

Don't Forget to Exercise.

Exercise is useful in imagining worry. Exercise releases brain chemicals that counteract anxiety and low mood. It also offers time away from worries and drives off "nervous energy." It is advised that people at least exercise half-hour a day of cardio exercise.

Practice Relaxation and Self-Care Techniques

It is important to highlight that most of these signs of emotional stress, worry, and anxiety are linked to one's mindset. Hence, if you want to release the anxious feelings you might be experiencing, you may need to practice some effective relaxation approaches. For example, relaxation techniques tend to serve the need of boosting one's art of thinking, and it helps reduce the tension that one might be experiencing. Some of the relaxation techniques that have proved to work include meditation as well as progressive muscle relaxation. Some of these approaches don't need a company or many individuals for them to be effective. Techniques like yoga can be done in the comfort of your living room and accomplish excellent results. But, it's important to know some of these activities you need to carry out in life.

Chapter 7: Good Habit Formation

"Who do you want to be and what do you want to do with your life?"

Those are the two fundamental questions you need to answer as you start to form the basis of good habits. It's no secret that humans are creatures of habit. Research shows that about 40-50% of our daily behavior is based on habit. That's a big percentage. That means nearly half of all that you do each day is a habit. For example, if you wake up at the same time each day, that's a habit. Brushing your teeth in the morning when you wake up and at the end of the day before going to bed, that's a habit. Going home from work every day and enjoying an hour relaxing on the sofa with a snack and your favorite Netflix film, that's a routine. Spending 10-minutes a day meditating, that's a habit too. Driving a car, checking our phones several times a day, responding to emails, grabbing a cup of coffee from your regular barista on the way to work, the list of habits could stretch forever.

By definition, habits are automated behaviors that we repeatedly carry out and always within the same context or environment. We're so used to going through the motions that these habits run in our subconscious mind. This means even though you might not be consciously aware of what you're doing it anymore, it doesn't matter because you've done it so many times that you don't have to pay attention to the behavior anymore. There are bad habits, and there are good ones. Overthinking is one example of a bad habit that you're trying to break out of right now. When our thoughts run on autopilot through the subconscious mind, that's when we tend to engage in overthinking. Our minds are wandering, we're thinking about the past, what's going to happen a few hours from now, what's going to happen next week perhaps. You may be going through all the right steps of your habit, but you're not really.

"Present."

Let's go back to the example of driving a car. Have you ever experienced those moments when you're driving the way you always do, but once you get to your destination and switch your mind back to the present, you can't really recall how you got there? Driving and following the commands of the GPS have become so habitual you don't think about what you're doing at all. A cue usually triggers the habits we perform in an environment you're always in. For example, brushing your teeth is a habit that gets triggered the moment you get out of bed in the morning and make your way to the bathroom. At night, it's triggered by the knowledge that you're going to bed, and this is what needs to happen before you do. A habit becomes easier to stick to when there's a reward at the end. When you spend 30-minutes a day on the treadmill, you're motived by the fresh fruit smoothie that's waiting for you at the end of your workout session. Or when you're hard at work all day and look forward to coming back home, knowing that you'll be rewarded by the comfy pajamas you get to put on as you flick through your latest Netflix selection.

It doesn't matter what the reward waiting at the end of the habit is as long as dopamine is present. When dopamine is discharged into your brain, you feel good, and that feeling makes you want to keep to that routine. When the brain is struck by dopamine, he says, "I like this, it feels amazing," and he needs to keep doing it again. Your mobile phones are the easiest example to illustrate this point. Every time your phone beeps or lights up with a new notification, you get a small hit of dopamine in the brain. Social media companies have cleverly made their platforms so addictive, so it keeps you coming back for more. It feels good to get those notifications coming in. it feels good to see other people reacting and commenting on the content you've shared. Most of us couldn't last a day without our mobile phones on our side. These devices have become so habitual to spend a day without it would feel as though we were missing a limb. It just wouldn't feel complete.

In his book, The Power of Habit, Charles Duhigg talks about an interesting concept called "The Habit Loop."

The cue triggers the routine, the routine triggers the reward, and the reward triggers the cue. Because the brain likes the reward that it gets, it keeps repeating the same behavior when the cue comes up just to feel that burst of pleasure again. That's essentially what the habit loop is, and we repeat these behaviors many times on several occasions. The question is, how do we effectively break the bad habits and start replacing them with better ones instead?

The human brain is complex. When you repeat a certain behavior for a prolonged period, a set of neurons in your brain start connecting. In the beginning, this connection is weak since the habit is still new. After several weeks of repeating the same behavior, the connections begin to get thicker and stronger. This is probably around the time when you find you're not struggling as much as you were, in the beginning, to carry out this new habit. The more you repeat this new behavior, the stronger the connections become. Going back to the example of exercise. Yes, it feels like a massive struggle in the beginning. You've probably had to literally drag yourself to the gym or force yourself to go through a workout. It feels hard; it feels unfamiliar; it even feels almost painful to be wrestling against yourself like this. But after several weeks and months of repeatedly exercising three or four times a week, it doesn't feel so hard anymore. You begin to look forward to going to the gym and getting a good workout in for the day. After several months or a year of doing this, it starts to feel strange, not exercising because you've become so used to it.

The brain is an energy consumer. It needs to be fed with the right kind of energy to be efficient. It processes a lot of info each day from the stimuli we're exposed to, and to make its function as efficient as possible, the brain needs to choose the most important behaviors that cost the least amount of energy. The thicker the neuron connections in your brain are, the less energy it needs to behave. The exercise example starts to feel easier after several months because your brain recognizes this as an important activity to you, given that you made an effort to stick to it and see it through. It doesn't need to invest quite as much energy as it did in the beginning to ensure this habit sticks. The brain has almost 100 billion neurons, each connected by trillions of connections. It is complex, but despite the complexity, if you repeat a behavior often enough to become a habit, your brain starts recognizing this as important behavior. You'll be met with a lot less struggle.

The repeated behaviors you go through daily, no matter what they may be, is training your brain to decide what's important. It doesn't matter if the behavior is good or bad for you, or even if it's necessary, whenever repetition and dopamine are present, the brain will decide that the habit you're carrying out is important enough to stick around.

Why Good Habits Help

Psychologist William James once famously said: Make an ally out of your nervous system instead of making it an enemy. Nearly all good habits will start difficult in the beginning if you're not used to it. Regardless of whether it's good for you or not, your mind and body will probably reject it in the initial stages because it feels unfamiliar. In the beginning, you might think, "I really hate this. I don't want to do this anymore," but if you persist, after a while, that becomes "This isn't so bad. I can do this again today". The brain cannot differentiate what's good for you and what's bad. It is up to us to make that decision, which means we need to start actively building and reinforcing good habits that cancel out or replace the bad.

With all good habits, take small steps. Make tiny changes in the beginning if you need to. That tiny change will turn into a bigger change. Real change is always going to take time; this includes breaking away from the habit of overthinking. What you need to be is consistent and patient. These two keywords are going to be your secrets to succeeding at this new habit formation. Your habits play a big part in who you are today. You need to cultivate good habits, the ones that lead you one step closer to your goal and one step closer to the person you want to be. Changing your habits could completely change the course of your life.

The Greek philosopher Aristotle left us with a few wise words: "We are what we repeatedly do. Therefore, excellence is not an act. It's a habit." Chinese philosopher had some wise words about habits too when he said: "Men's natures are alike. What separates them is their habits." The people who live the most fulfilling lives know what matters to them. They know what's important, and they prioritize that above everything else, including trying to please others and live up to someone else's expectations. They live happy lives because they've crafted their life around what matters to them, thereby ensuring that their priorities are always at the center of everything they do. They have made it their purpose to live in a way where they can develop into the best version of themselves. How do we emulate what they do?

By crafting our lives around good habits. A good habit routine is one of the most powerful tools you can access to live a meaningful life. Routines help to bridge the gap between strategy and action, turning your goals into reality. Routines and good habits offer several benefits, including constraining our choices, so the number of choices we see at any given time is limited, which is great news for what you're attempting to do right now as you work on trying to get rid of your overthinking habit. Constrained choices help keep you progressing on the right path, leading to the second benefit they offer: Enable action. Good habits and a routine give us the momentum we need to keep moving forward. When you know where you're heading and what you're doing, things start to make sense, and that diminishes the likelihood of overthinking based on uncertainty and fear. Good habits and routines give your life meaning and a purpose. It gives you stability, which is something overthinkers need to help quiet that noisy mind.

Good habits matter because most people find it difficult to sustain motivation. When good habits are present, you don't need to rely on motivation as much when you're so accustomed to carrying out the behavior anyway. Going back once again to the example of exercising. Those who have made exercising a regular habit no longer need to force themselves to find the motivation and the willpower to get to the gym or do a quick workout from wherever they are. They simply do it. Compare that to someone who is just getting started trying to incorporate regular exercise into their routine. The struggle is genuine, and they often find themselves in a battle of wills between forcing themselves to workout and wanting to skip it altogether. Good habits make the difficult parts feel easier, which is one of the many reasons they matter. If you cultivated the good habit of thinking positive and training your mind to focus on the positives, it's easier to start cutting back on the excessive thoughts that run rampant in your mind.

You can train your mind to do anything, even the things that initially feel impossible. You can train your mind to wake up early. You can train yourself to go on that six-mile hike. You can train your mind to keep the negativity at bay. The initial stages of starting a good habit are the most important. You can't rely on motivation alone to get you through the tough first few weeks since motivation comes and goes. If a habit is fun, it's easier to stick to, but if it's a challenging habit like trying to shift your thinking from negative to positive, that's significantly harder to do.

Motivating Yourself to Change Your Habits

Everyone has some behavior that they would like to change about themselves. In this case, overthinking. Maybe someone you love is struggling with negative thoughts and overthinking, and you'd like to help them overcome it. So what do we need to get us to change our behavior? When you look at health campaigns that come with bold warning labels like Smoking Kills, Motorists Beware!, Don't Be Ignorant! Drinking Is Not a Joke, what do these campaign taglines have in common? They're all trying to scare you into changing your behavior. Warning messages are a common theme in policies too. Why do they employ this tactic? It's because there is a belief that if you "threaten" people enough and play on their fears, they'll be motivated to act in the way that you want them to. It seems like a logical strategy, but do you heed the warnings you see if you're honest with yourself? Probably not. They probably have minimal impact on you, and you forget about them as soon as you walk past those campaign posters. If the graphic images on smoke packets are not enough to deter smokers from smoking anyway, that's saying something about this attempted scare tactic. It's not effective enough.

Why do warnings have such little impact? Let's look at this from another perspective. When you induce fear in someone, two things are going to happen. They're either going to flee, or they're going to fight (the fight or flight response). Another response that gets triggered in the face of fear is that the person freezes. When we're confronted with something that we fear, our body and mind can shut down to limit the negative emotions generated. That's why some people are frozen in fear, rooted on the spot, unable to run or fight. Do we change our habits in the face of fear? No, we don't. That's probably the last thing on our minds at the time. Any negative emotion makes us feel bad, so we try to avoid it altogether rather than face it head-on. In the many facets of our lives, warning signs are indicating bad behavior.

People tend to change their beliefs if they know they are moving toward a more desirable option. The human mind is a fickle thing too. We tend to easily take in information that we want to hear and struggle to accept the news we don't want to hear. It doesn't matter what age group you belong to either. Whether you're in your 20s, 30,s 40s, 50s, 60s, and all the way up to as many years as you want to include in there, people will always easily take in the information they want to hear and reject the bad news they don't want to deal with. Therefore, instead of focusing or emphasizing the warnings about all the bad stuff that could happen in the future, you need to focus on the principles that will drive your mind and behavior toward positive change. Let's make a list of what these principles are:

Principle #1: Staying Positive

Overthinking and negative thoughts can leave you feeling at your lowest, more often than you should. Positive thinking is not the right way of thinking; it is a useful way of thinking. In this case, it's going to be used to help you overcome your overthinking. The Glass Half Empty or Half Full case is a classic example of what it takes to have a good outlook. You're not wrong by thinking of the glass as half full, but if you look at the glass as half empty and that makes you miserable, that's a negative thought that is working against you.

Positive thinking is about cultivating thoughts that make you feel better and happier about yourself. Going back to the dopamine example and how your brain craves for what makes it feel good. It's not enough to say "I want to be a positive thinker". If you don't understand why you need to become a positive thinker, it won't be long before you go ricocheting back to your old ways. But if you have a concrete reason why you need to cultivate this habit, there's a firm foundation for you to latch on to.

Why do you need to become a positive thinker? Because you deserve to be happy. Why do you need to encourage positive thoughts? Because they remind you that you can do anything you set your mind to. Why does positivity matter? Because it allows you to see the situations you're faced with in a new light. What's your reason, why?

Principle #2: Doing Your Best

No matter what you take on in life, if you always make it a point to give it your best, you will always get better results. That's a promise you can hold on to. Giving 100% in all that you do will eventually lead to greater things in life, even if you fail several times along the way. When you fall, the only way you stay down is if you don't make an effort to stand up again. The ones who go above and beyond are the ones who almost always become successful. Those who work hard, study hard, and train hard will always get more out of their life than those who take it easy, and that's the motivation you need to start making "do your best" a habit you carry with you all day and every day.

Do your best, and give it all that you got. That way, if it still doesn't work out, at least you can take pride in knowing that you tried. Even in failure, you still reap the benefits in the form of life lessons that you can take with you to the next challenge so that when you try again, this time, you get one step further than you did the last time. Overthinking will make you doubt yourself and try to squash you down, but you need to push back against that. When it feels hard to give it your best effort, that's when you need to push even harder. The pain will always be temporary, but the results will live with you forever.

Principle #3: Learning to Be Aware and Knowing What You Want

Decision-making is the force that will shape your destiny. But before you can reach the point of making decisions without overthinking, you need to be aware and know what you want out of life. Every decision you have made has led you to this moment where you are now. If you had made a different decision back, then your life might have turned out completely different.

When you know what you want out of life, making decisions becomes easier. When you're aware of where you are in life and where you want to be, the right decisions become that much clearer. That sense of purpose and a goal lifts the cloud of uncertainty that overthinking causes because you can say, "I know what I want, and this is what I need to do." It's like driving a car. You rarely ever start driving without a specific destination in mind. In this case, your destination is to overcome your excessive thoughts. Where are you right now? Still struggling to overcome your excessive thoughts. How are you going to get from where you are to where you want to be? By forming good habits and using all the strategies, you'll learn as you progress through the rest of this book.

Principle #4: Ensuring You're In the Right State of Mind

Think about all the most challenging and difficult times in your life. Back then, you probably thought of these as your most "unfortunate" moments. Yet, now, if you traced back the ripple effects that came out of those moments, a lot of these moments turn out to be the best thing that could have happened to you at the time. These moments gave you your greatest strength and growth. So perhaps we shouldn't be so quick to dismiss challenges as negative moments from now on.

Assuring you're in the right state of mind means thinking with clarity, away from the noise and the distractions your overthinking tendencies try to plow you with. Being in the right state of mind and thinking clearly allows you to see that emotional reactions are unnecessary most of the time. That a lot of your worry could easily be handled if you thought with a clear head. To change your habits:

Start training your mind to see these challenges as opportunities.

See them as a chance to grow, to increase your resilience, to test what you're capable of and how far you can go.

See every challenge you have as an opportunity, and your entire perspective will shift.

Principle #5: Quitting Perfectionism

Novelist and writer Anne Lamott eloquently put it when she said: Perfectionism is the voice of the oppressor, and it is the enemy of people. Now, perfectionism is not all bad, but if you're an over-thinker, this is one habit you need to rid yourself off because of the constant pressure you face to meet unrealistic standards. Tasks seem a lot more monumental when perfectionism is a factor, and what you get in return is stress and anxiety from overthinking every little detail.

This habit becomes easier to break once you come to terms with the fact that you're not perfect, and neither is anyone else. This statement might be hard to accept at first, especially when the internet constantly presents us with perfectionism ideals. People who show off their success on social media are proud to show you the finished product, but they never show you the hours of hard work and failed attempts that went into the process before they reached that point. Success is never possible without mistakes along the way, and that's a fact you can hold to as you work on freeing yourself from the pressure to be perfect.

Principle #6: Creating A To-Do List

Creating a to-do list reminds you that you're capable of getting a lot done in a day, which is a problem overthinkers struggle with. They invest a lot of time in fretting and worrying about how to get things done or what they should get started. Every task feels urgent when there's no structure to it, and that's where to-do lists come in handy. When you look at your to-do list and see all the tasks you've crossed off for the day, there's a sense of accomplishment that comes from it. You were probably so busy during the day that you ignore how much you're actually getting done until you look back at your list and say, "Wow! I did all that!".

A to-do list gives you a sense of direction and gives your day a purpose. When you've got a list on hand, you know exactly what must be done. Even better if you allocate time blocks next to the tasks you've written on your list. It tells your overthinking brain, "Okay, I need to get this done within an hour," and that self-imposed deadline pushes you to forget everything else for a while to focus on what needs to get done. Distractions are another common problem faced by overthinkers, and it's easy to get distracted when you've got nothing to guide you. Your to-do list then becomes your daily guiding compass, and once you make it a habit to stick to the lists you create, your confidence increases along with your efficiency. This also happens to be great for cultivating the positive mindset you need because of the sense of accomplishment that accompanies each completed task.

Principle #7: Social Incentives

We're social creatures by nature, and we care about what other people are doing. You might want to do the same thing they do in some instances, but you want to do it better. Others' opinions are strong enough to make you conform or submit to peer pressure because you want to fit in, and you want to be accepted. The fear of social rejection sends a shockwave through your brain that is strong enough to kick start its overthinking drive. In overcoming excessive thoughts, this principle could be used to your advantage.

Highlighting what other people are doing can act as a strong social incentive to create new good habits. For example, if you knew that 9 out of 10 people in your office were thinking positively, which group would you want to be in? Naturally, you'll want to be part of the group of 9. No one wants to feel singled out, and that incentive could be the push you need to start adopting positive thought habits. Who do you know within your immediate social circle that is practicing great habits you admire? Maybe they always see the bright side even though they've gone through some of the toughest situations, you know. Maybe they've always got a smile on their faces even on the hardest days when everything feels like a struggle. Maybe you're in awe of how they manage to stay so calm under stressful situations that would cause your brain to go into overdrive. Whoever they may be, what they should be is your role model. Create that desire within you to want to be like them.

Principle #8: Instant Gratification

Immediate rewards are satisfying. Indulging in your bad habits feels good; that's why you want to keep doing them. The "reward" or effect that you see from these bad habits is almost instantaneous at times, which makes it the more appealing option. We place more value on rewards that we can get now instead of rewards that you might get in the future. The future is so far away. After all, who has the patience to wait that long? The overthinking "here-and-now" version of yourself would rather choose tangible results they can enjoy right away instead of waiting for the uncertainty you're bound to face in the future if you waited.

You could now use this approach to your advantage when trying to get yourself to adopt more positive mental habits. Creating little rewards to look forward to will make it more likely that you're going to stick to this new habit of yours. Associating positive thinking with a reward you look forward to will make it less likely you're going to allow negative thinking to run rampant in your mind any longer.

Principle #9: Monitoring Your Progress

You need to be held culpable for your actions. The problem is we don't do this often enough; that's why we let a lot of negative habits slide under the radar. This includes the tendency to overthink nearly everything. But if you held yourself responsible for all the times overthinking landed you in trouble, you'd be motivated enough to start tracking your progress. With challenge comes the best kind of change, but you won't know which areas you're struggling in unless you identify what they are.

Tracking how well you're doing might sound like a tedious task, but it is one of the most effective ways to highlight your progress rather than your decline. Tracking your progress also enables you to see which areas hold even more opportunities for better change to take place. After all, if you want to live the best version of yourself, you need to know how well you're doing so you understand what areas need to be fixed. Moreover, keeping tabs on your progress gives you one extra benefit that all overthinkers crave. It gives you a sense of control. When you're in charge of your progress or decline, which way do you want to see yourself swinging?

Chapter 8: Clarify Your New Life Priorities

Define Your Life Priorities

Once you have outlined your key values, these values will help you complete an exercise that will improve your life. Define your life priorities so that you can spend your time, money, and energy.

Without understanding our priorities, we let the pressure of life to guide our actions and decisions. An attractive offer comes, and we purchase it. Someone interrupts our workflow, and we permit it. When we don't know the bigger "why" of our lives, there are no boundaries to help us.

Below is an exercise to help you determine where you are spending money, energy, and time.

How much time per day do you think you waste on irrelevant activities not connected to your main values?

How are you connecting with people you care about unconsciously?

How do you make life decisions?

How are you using money unconsciously?

What obligations, tasks, and connections are you letting in your life unconsciously?

How are you neglecting other critical parts of your life that you tend to have no time for?

Now that you have an idea of how much you are using your energy and concentration let's explore the right way to prioritize your life's critical areas.

Let's look at seven sections of your life that will help you determine your priorities and how you want to use time and money.

If you want to eliminate any of these areas, please do so if they don't apply to you.

The areas of your life include:

1.   Family

2.   Marriage

3.   Self-improvement

4.   Leisure

5.   Life management

6.   Career

7.   Health and fitness

If you sleep 8 hours a day, you are going to be left with 16 waking hours. Now, let's set aside 2 hours for personal hygiene activities and eating. Then you will be left with 14 hours. In a week, that translates to 98 hours per week.

In a typical world, how can you prioritize those seven areas of your life? How many hours in a week are you ready to commit to each sector?

It's good to start with the priority to make the most positive difference in your life or where you feel the most imbalance. You might find this section reflecting one or more of your values that you aren't honoring.

For instance, you may have a core value associated with family and life priority of spending enough time with your family. Start small by deciding to include an extra hour a week spending time with your family.

Of course, this will affect some other tasks, but you should ensure it affects tasks that are not a big priority.

Keep adding weekly time to your life priorities until you have them reorganized to match your ideal.

Sometimes, altering a priority can be hard. If you want to spend more time with your kids and wife, it will affect your work schedule? If yes, what do you need to take charge of any fallout?

If you want to concentrate more on your health and fitness, you will need to develop challenging habits to follow through on this priority.

If you want to experience a healthy marriage, you might need to give up time in front of the TV or the computer, which might be hard at first.

Simply defining your life priorities isn't enough. You need to take the difficult actions necessary to make the changes you want to see in your life. However, the closer you come to your real goal, the less internal battles you will feel.

As time goes, you won't miss those old habits, behaviors, and choices. Your life will flow more easily because you are living authentically, true to your priorities and values.

Step 3: Concentrate on Mindful Goal Setting

A natural result of setting priorities and having values is thinking about how they apply to your life in the future. While worrying about the future leads to an unsettled mind, planning for the future is a critical and valuable aspect that can set the stage for true satisfaction for the years to come.

Well, it's possible to look forward to a better future and remain happy with your life right now? Can you be satisfied and change at the same time? We know it's possible to concentrate on the future while still learning how to enjoy the current moment.

The realities of our lives are constantly pushing us into the future. We are anxious about paying the bills, how our children will turn out whether we will remain healthy. And the way of setting goals is future-oriented.

Longing and fighting against what causes suffering. Hoping for more, for something different, for something better at the expense of contentment in the current status denies us of life.

But remember that change will come whether or not you choose to focus.

Change is a must, whether we are sitting or wringing our hands about some imagined future results. So we might as well define our futures mindfully.

Once you acknowledge the truth that contentment and change can take place simultaneously, you decrease the tension between wondering it's an either-or proposition. There's a means to create a balance between self-creation and mindfulness.

You can check the process of creating and fulfilling your goals as a place for happiness and contentment. Instead of holding back happiness while you wait for a result, enjoy every stage along the path. Every small effort toward your goals should be celebrated.

Let's see how to create and strive toward your goals in a manner that supports the bigger "why" of your life.

When you first sit down and focus on your career goals, bear in mind that your fundamental beliefs and life preferences are useful as a focal point. As long as your beliefs and objectives remain true, they should be a roadmap to your goals. If not, brace yourself for the future of regret and unhappiness.

Step 4. Define SMART Goals

The easiest way to focus on what is important in life is to define SMART goals.

Set goals for each quarter instead of a yearlong goal that usually takes you out of the current moment.

Your goals should be Smart, Measurable, Achievable, Relevant, and Time-bound.

Step 5: Connect Goals to Your Passions

Most people live desperate lives. They wake up with a low-level sense of anxiety. At work, they feel underrated and undermined. And when they arrive home, they feel physically and mentally tired, with just enough energy to cook, take care of the family, and spend a few hours watching television. Then they sleep and wake up to do the same thing.

While this may not describe you exactly, you can still relate. We all accept less than our dreams. We remain in jobs that don't motivate us or make us happy. All this adds to our mental clutter.

Life has a means of eating us, and before we discover, we're already far down a path that doesn't look what we want for our lives. By the time we discover it, we have duties that add another reason to maintain the status quo-even if we hate it.

The fact is that your mental health can be destroyed when you feel unsatisfied with your work. Consider the amount of negative mental energy you have subjected to a bad boss or a career move you regret. We spend a lot of time working. Therefore, the decision you make about your job will have the ability to make or break your general happiness.

If you get a job that you love, not only will this free your mind from oppressive thoughts but will also feel energized in parts of your life.

Well, What Does it Mean to Live Your Passion?

It can be defined using a few examples.

You have a high sense of self-confidence and motivation about what you're doing because it is best for you.

You feel like you are in the perfect place, doing something in your work or life that feels authentic to who you are and how you're wired.

Your entire life is better, and your relationships are happier because you are more self-directed and present in your work.

You attract interesting, like-minded people in your life and work.

Discovering your passion and making it part of your life is not something that happens immediately. It is not like teaching you how to follow a recipe or drive a car. It involves different actions and experiments to figure everything out.

Chapter 9: Benefits of Decluttering Your Mind

One of the most notable reasons you want to declutter your mind is that it already plays a negative role in your life. You may be experiencing its effect right now and may want to do something about it.

Most of the available resources we find online and in print when we look for help point out dealing with a cluttered mind's effects. This is just like traditional medicine nowadays, which uses treatment to deal with the symptoms and not cause the symptoms.

All these pieces of advice have a valid point. But in the end, if you look carefully at the bigger picture, you have to admit that something is missing. No matter how hard you try and succeed in tackling the symptoms that derive from a cluttered mind, you will need to address the central issue you are facing eventually. Your account is slowly and steadily becoming your enemy – the cluttering creeps in, step by step, and only by realizing and reversing this process will you be able to put an end to this spiral of unhappiness.

The benefits derived from dealing with the cause rather than the effects are enormous.

Being Efficient

It is inconceivable not to notice that many of us who try to deal with problems we're facing in our day-to-day life have limited amounts of energy to spend. We all have to be productive, stay healthy, take care of others that rely on us for their well-being; and at the same time, we have a job or are searching for a job, we are part of a family or a relationship, we have our dreams, desires, needs.

The obvious question arises: is it worth fighting to deal with our problems in such a way that we spend a great deal of time and resources? Does this struggle end eventually? Are we efficient? I'm afraid the honest answer is not a positive one.

Vicious Circle

As I mentioned before, most of the available resources for those who strive to achieve happiness in their lives are limited to dealing with the symptoms and not the cause. Moreover, we can observe a pattern that develops. How so?

When we approach an issue that is causing distress by tackling the problem in itself, not only do we lose perspective, but we enter a merry-go-round that takes up a lot of effort and energy and gives us the illusion that we are advancing towards our goal. After we deal with social anxiety by making new friends, the next issue presents itself, for we've spent a lot of money and time, and now we felt insecure and stressed over our cost on day-to-day living. If we work more to cover those new expenses, we end up stressed, tired, unable to maintain the relationships we just developed, and hence we get a new form of social anxiety. And even worse, we feel disappointed, and we blame ourselves for that.

Stop. Take a Step Back. Unclutter Your Mind.

We just don't know it could be done with little effort. We have no idea that we stand close to the solution, for we cannot examine the correct obstacles. Keep in mind that hardly anyone can do this on his or her own. Knowledge is power, but at the same time, learning is shared and accumulated not as limited by individuals, but as a collective mind that continually improves.

For now, you already feel the answer to the "Why declutter your mind?" question. So, let's engage in building up the whole perspective.

When you clear out mental clutter and its symptoms, it can make you feel as if you are peeling onions.

Imagine yourself trying to peel off all the onion layers so that you can get to the core. This is what decluttering does to your mind. It peels back all your thoughts and ideas. You peel away that which your cluttered thoughts made you believe to get down to your truth.

Everyone has experienced moments of profound love, peace, connection, and clarity once all the layers are peeled away. These moments occur when the mind is already clutter-free.

Anyway, before you learn about the exercises that eliminate negative thinking, you should understand why you have such thoughts. The following are the most common causes of mental clutter: Daily Stress.

Too much stress is the main reason why so many people feel overwhelmed. In fact, stress caused by information overload, endless options, and physical clutter can trigger various mental health issues, including depression, anxiety, and panic attacks.

What's going on inside your mind? How does it make you feel? Could it be that maybe - just maybe - the way you feel has a lot to do with the physical stuff you're surrounded with? Physical possessions are more than just the stuff that surrounds your external environment? They are a manifestation of what is going on inside your mind. Your phone bills. Your laundry. Your cabinets and shelves full of unused items, stuff you may have even forgotten that you own. The couches and chairs piled with old papers, books, and magazines in the corner gathering dust. The unnecessary, non-essential items in your life take up so much room and space that they start to feel like a burden weighing down.

Experts believe that the average human mind is full of what they call mental clutter. They call it an "unbearable burden" that we all carry yet don't realize the direct link with our external surroundings. We've become so accustomed to the noisy "chatter" in our minds that we start to think of them as normal. It's now "normal" to feel stressed out. It's "normal" to think more than a dozen worrying, stressful thoughts at a time. Our inability to organize our thoughts in our heads is manifesting externally. If you stop to look - really look - at what your immediate environment looks like, ask yourself this one question: How much of these items do you need?

A lot of the items that we own are, truth be told, not essential. You don't need the same shirt in multiple colors. You don't need 10 pairs of jeans when you keep wearing the only two because you like those best. You don't need several books lined up on the bookshelves if you have no interest in ever rereading them. Most people are drowning in their own clutter, and they don't even know it. The average American has 300,000 items in their home. Piles of letters, mail, and magazines in one corner, papers, documents Expired food in the fridge, closets bursting full of clothes, some of which you may not have worn in over a year or even forgotten about. Old shoes, souvenirs, and mementos you've had since your childhood, gifts you've received over the years but never used. Come on, now, be honest. Do you need this much stuff?

Understanding Clutter and Decluttering

Your home is not the only thing that is susceptible to clutter. In fact, a cluttered mind and a cluttered home are the same. For example, holding onto clutter is the same as holding onto the past. You have it hard to let go of some items, even when you know you should because of the sentimental value and the memories attached to it. Sometimes you don't even want to get rid of it because it was a gift, and you're worried about hurting the other person's feelings. You know you're never going to use it, but you hold onto it anyway. Holding onto items that are no longer of any use to you will stop you from moving forward because you can't look ahead when you're constantly looking back. It's the same thing when your mind is cluttered. You hold onto the past because you can't bring yourself to let go, you keep having the same thoughts over and over again, and you have a hard time letting go of certain memories that hurt, even when you know that you should.

Understanding physical clutter is a lot easier than understanding mental clutter. With physical clutter, we can see it. We know clutter is referring to the piles and stacks of unnecessary items we have around the home. Mental clutter is a little harder to define. Have you ever had days when you feel so frazzled? Like your mind is being pulled in a million different directions, and you feel exhausted from the sheer energy you've had to expand thinking and to process the thoughts you have? On any given day, the average person has about 60,000 to 80,000 thoughts running through our minds. That's approximately 2,500 to 3,300 thought that you're churning out in an hour. Other experts believe that number may be slightly smaller, an average of 50,000 thoughts a day perhaps. That's still a big number, and what's worse, more than half of the thoughts you have are not beneficial. Most of the thought is either useless or unimportant, which means they take up all that space in your mind of nothing.

Our brain is active and constantly on the move, like a butterfly flitting from one beautiful flower to the next, never stopping to stand still long enough. Thinking is such an automatic process that we don't realize our thoughts unless something significant grabs our attention. We're completely oblivious to how these thoughts take up too much space in our mind, making it difficult to focus and concentrate, nothing but a distraction, taking your attention away from what you should be focusing on in your life instead. The time and hours you spend thinking unnecessary thoughts could be put to better use doing something productive, something that will bring you one step closer to your goals. A cluttered mind distracts you from what's important in life, taking up more of your attention and time than it should.

What is a cluttered mind? It is a mind that:

Has a confusing thought process

Can't operate in a calm, productive, and focused manner

That struggles to stay positive.

That struggles to hold on to happiness.

That is full of thoughts that don't contribute in a positive way to your life or well-being.

Is lacking direction

Ruminates too much

Obsesses about what is beyond your control

Has a hard time letting go of negativity, resentment, and anger

Can be easily swayed by circumstances, opinions, and criticism

Easily distracted by external circumstances.

In short, a cluttered mind results in a negative mindset. The most dangerous thing about a cluttered mindset is that you're relinquishing control. You're giving up control of your life by letting your thoughts dictate what you should think and how you should feel. You forget that you are the one with the power to control your life, not your mind, and certainly not your thoughts. When you give up and leave it to your thoughts to decide your fate, when you no longer take responsibility for your thoughts and actions, that's a clear sign that something needs to change if you want to initiate any kind of change in your life for the better.

How Clutter Affects the Brain

If your brain were a computer, clutter would represent having too many tabs open in the brain at one time. It's messy, disorganized, and makes it hard to focus on anything.

Because there are so many thoughts taking place in our mind at any given time, when these thoughts are negative or contradict each other, they start to cause problems. These thoughts are partially responsible for the stress, anxiety, and depression that so many people are battling with today, not realizing how mental clutter has a part to play in it. When your thoughts begin affecting you in a very negative way, it's a real problem. Harboring negative emotions is a sign that your mind is cluttered. It starts with one thought, one feeling, and before you know it, you're sliding down a very slippery slope of unhappy emotions, and you don't know how to slow down anymore. Negativity puts your mind in a bad place you never want it to be in, and it can quickly strip you of any possibility of happiness.

Your brain is not designed to have its attention pulled in so many different directions. Your brain needs to be organized at peace. Focused on one thing at a time, preferably something positive and uplifting that makes you feel good. The trouble is, negativity is not entirely avoidable. There will be some moments in life that are less than pleasant. It's even worse when we lack the ability to properly organize and filter the information we receive, like your email inbox. If you don't delete or filter the important emails from the junk mail, everything is just going to pile together in one big mess, making your inbox too stressful to look at or even deal with. To say we're never going to feel the stressful effects of negativity would be a lie. We can't always avoid them, but what you can do is learn how to process them, assess them, and deal with them in better, healthier ways so they don't linger and clutter your mind.

Your mental habits are the reason you're not reaching your full potential. Your "busy" mind is the reason you feel "stuck," stressed, anxious, and overwhelmed so easily. Clutter is bad for your brain, and the negativity it causes is one of the most debilitating hindrances you can have, taking up more than its fair share of space in your mind that there is no room for anything else. Don't forget about the physical clutter that is secretly affecting you in the background, too, without you knowing it. There's a saying that goes: "Mess equals stress," and there's an excellent reason why. Being surrounded by disorganization makes it hard for anyone to concentrate. We are so conditioned to a life of materialism that we genuinely believe the decisions about the purchases we make are based on careful thought and sound logic. We make excuses and give reasons as to why we need to purchase more stuff. We make purchases hoping that we will finally become a happier version of ourselves, but we become unhappy when that doesn't happen. The emotions we feel only aggravate the mental clutter that is already there.

What Decluttering Is NOT

Decluttering is not just necessary; it's satisfying: just imagine to feel like an immense weight has been lifted off, your mind is liberating. Your mind is not an abandoned attic. It's not a place you can come and dump your thoughts, hoping they will either go away on their own or that you'll forget about them. The emotions, dreams, goals, unfulfilled desires, memories are all still going to be there, and they'll continue to be there until you find a way to process and organize the thoughts you have properly. When you spring clean your home, doesn't it make you feel good to toss out all that unnecessary junk? That's the same thing you need to do with your mind. Toss out all the unnecessary and organize what remains.

Mental Decluttering Is: Confronting Your Feelings

Sweeping them under the rug is not going to work. That strategy has never worked, and it never will. Avoidance and denial are two coping mechanisms you need to leave behind because trying to conceal your emotions will only lead to emotional and mental fatigue. The thought of confronting your unpleasant emotions sounds dreadful, but it is a necessary part of the decluttering process. Suppressing your emotions prevents your brain from doing a good job of thinking clearly.

Mental Decluttering Is Not: Avoiding Worry Altogether

Like negativity, worry is not something you can avoid entirely. There will be moments where you are bound to worry, it's an inevitable part of life. Mental decluttering is not about running away or trying to deny and block out worry altogether, but to be more proactive about it. Instead of letting the worry take over your entire day, keep your mind organized by allowing yourself time to worry before returning to your other tasks. In between tasks, pick a time that works best, and schedule 5 to 10 minutes specifically for your worries.

There is always going to be something to worry about. You can't avoid worry forever, so what you're doing to do instead is to be more proactive about it. Instead of letting the worry take over your entire day, keep your mind organized by allowing yourself time to worry before returning to your other tasks. Rehash your concerns, but think about solutions instead of distorting those thoughts and making yourself feel worse. Train your brain to be solution-oriented instead of circling over the same worry repeatedly. This keeps the worries from spinning out of control and distracting you throughout the day so you can still stay on top of everything you need to do and process your worries without neglecting them.

Mental Decluttering Is: Tidying Up Your Environment

The environment you spend the most time in is going to have the greatest effect on your psyche. It's not a good thing that we have become so used to our environment being noisy, hectic, stressful, and messy that we don't even notice it anymore. There's a good chance at least one area (if not several) of your home that is cluttered with far too much stuff.

How did it get to such an extent? Well, for one thing, most of us are far too busy these days, rushing from one appointment to the next. We spend long days at the office, and by the time we get home, we're too exhausted to do anything else. Also, cleaning is not exactly an activity many look forward to, and when you procrastinate and keep putting off cleaning the mess around your home, that's how clutter starts to build. The bigger the mess, the longer it is going to take you to clean. A 5-minute cleanup is now going to take 2-3 hours to get done when the mess has grown far too big. Both your home and your mind are like a boat on the ocean. Keep pilling clutter in that boat it will eventually sink to the bottom under the weight of it all.

Mental Decluttering Is Not: Limited to Materialistic Possessions

Decluttering is not limited to removing the excess physical items around your home. In fact, mental decluttering encompasses all aspects of your life. Everything that we're exposed to, everything we do, everything we say or think affects the brain in one way or another. Mental decluttering is also about eliminating toxic relationships, old ideas, and bad habits. Anything in your environment that is negative needs to be eliminated. This includes any toxic individuals who happen to be in your life.

Can Decluttering Change Your Life?

It's hard to make a fresh start when your old worries still maintain their hold on you. Every new year, most people begin with a list of new year resolutions enthusiastically prepared. Motivations run high, and we all intend to keep see these resolutions through in the end. But as the year goes on, the initial excitement slowly wanes, and we find ourselves slipping back into old habits. Slowly, the lack of motivation begins creeping into the other areas of your life. You find it hard to get anything done, and productivity is running low, you're easily distracted, you feel tired all the time, you've lost your sense of purpose, and thoughts of the past still haunt you. Without decluttering your mind, you'll be trapped in this toxic cycle of thought forever, wasting several good years of your life feeling unhappy.

Decluttering mentally (and physically) is going to change your life. Clutter is unnecessary work, and unnecessary work only leads to stress. It's a burden to take on more than you can handle, and when the mess gets so bad you feel overwhelmed, there's only one thing left to do. Free yourself. Clutter is distracting and annoying, causing far too much negativity that we don't need. Instead of agonizing, it's time to start organizing. Besides the obvious benefit of having a cleaner environment and a happier mind, decluttering is the solution you've been looking for, and this is why it's going to benefit your life:

More Room for What Matters - Purging the unnecessary out of your life, both physical and mental, you're creating space. That space makes you feel like you can breathe again. Accumulating physical items makes it even harder for us to let go, and we hold on to things sometimes not because of the memory attached to it but because we always think, "What if I need this tomorrow or next week or next year?". Be honest, though, how many times have you actually needed the items you're holding on to "just in case"? You already have everything you need to survive and be happy, and those are the items you use daily. If you're not using it regularly, you don't need it.

A Greater Sense of Happiness - With a better focus on what's important in life, mental and physical decluttering also brings you joy because you have a better focus on things that matter. You're more efficient, concentrate better, and you know what your priorities are. You find yourself enjoying life because you're now free from what was making you unhappy in the past.

Peace of Mind - A noisy mind is one that can never be at peace. How could you be when your thoughts are either making you anxious or worried or both. We create a lot of stress for ourselves, and the attachment to materialism certainly doesn't help matters either. Buying more stuff doesn't make us happy... maybe it does at the time of purchase, but that feeling soon fades away. Materialism is nothing more than trying to fill an empty void we don't want to deal with, and once you start embracing this reality, it's easier to let go of everything that weighs you down.

It Changes the Way You Think – It's hard to ever truly feel happy if you continue to anchor your happiness to external possessions. Decluttering your mind changes the way you think. You begin to find happiness from within instead of relying on materialism and frivolous world possessions that never last for long. When there are fewer distractions in your life, you will be able to shift your focus on what truly matters in your life. For example, your health, your well-being, your family, your friends, your partner, your spouse, your pets, your hobbies, your passion, and all the other things will start to take precedence once again in your life. These are the things that you should be valued more than how many shiny new objects or clothes you could purchase.

Greater Efficiency - Suddenly, you find yourself becoming a lot more efficient with a lot less stuff in your life than what you were before. You can concentrate better, your priorities more in focus, you find yourself feeling lighter, happier, and able to work a lot more efficiently and make more productive use of your time because you have fewer things around you that distract you. You will find yourself supervising your time more efficiently with fewer distractions, and you won't feel as pressured as you once did before because of this. You will be able to accomplish more, feel more productive, and won't feel as pressed for time as you once did because nothing is distracting you from what you should be doing.

Setting an Example for Future Generations - Whether you have kids right now or in the future, you'll be setting a good example when you live a simple, clutter-free, uncomplicated life. You'll teach them valuable life lessons, see those material possessions are not responsible for bringing you happiness and be happy and grateful for the things they already possess in their lives. It helps them to value what they have more and learn to distinguish between needs and wants.

Does Decluttering Help You Become a More Efficient Learner?

Yes, it does. The biggest productivity killer we're faced with today is distractions, even more so because we're carrying the primary source of distraction with us all day and every day. Our mobile phones. They also happen to be the cause of a lot of the mental clutter we deal with. Social media is one of the many culprits that make it difficult to focus long enough to learn any new skill. So, it makes sense that to enhance productivity and our learning capacity, we need to eliminate the distractions that make it hard.

Learning becomes easier with a clear purpose in your life and without the unnecessary distractions stealing your focus. With less mental clutter weighing on your mind, it paves the way for neuroplasticity to take place. Neuroplasticity is the foundation of learning, and it also creates an amazingly resilient brain in the process. Neuroplasticity is your brain's ability to change its physical structure and function based on life experiences, thoughts, emotions, and repetitive behaviors daily, whether good or bad, gets wired into our system, and the structure of our brain because of this ability. Learning to control our minds is one of the most difficult things we can do. It's easy to let our thoughts get the best of us, which is why it is so easy to be consumed by negativity, and external circumstances can affect us to such an extent. Want to create a happier life? Start by getting rid of anything unhelpful for your brain.

Chapter 10: How to Manage Stress, Anxiety, and Depression

It is fascinating to learn that our thoughts define what happens to us. From a psychological perspective, it means that we can control what happens to us by simply learning how to control our thoughts. This is a powerful technique, indeed. Knowing that you have power over what happens to you is something that most people are unaware of. The reality is that you become what you think. If you look closely, whatever happens to you, good or bad, stems from your thoughts.

What you think about affects your mental health and wellbeing. Your thoughts lead to the emotional state that you might be experiencing. Often, this will affect your health. If your thoughts are preoccupied with sad events, then the chances are that you will constantly feel sad. If you constantly think about the fun activities you engage in with your friends, you attract the same energy to your life. From this, you will garner deeper insight into why your thoughts could be identified as the cause for your dwindling productivity at work, lack of sleep, and your failing social relationships.

The Law of Attraction

If you are concerned about your life's direction, then the law of attraction may be a useful tool to get you back on track. You might conclude that this is a law that helps you attract things around you on the surface. Well, just as the name suggests, this is a powerful law that suggests that you attract what you focus on. Believe it or not, this law is always working to shape your life. What people don't understand is that they are constantly shaping their lives consciously or subconsciously. The life that you have today is attributed to what you thought about years ago. Sure, you might not get exactly what you wanted, but you will be better off than thinking negatively.

Your future is shaped by the way you think and the way you respond to situations today. Therefore, if you think that the coming months will be difficult for you, rest assured that they are more likely to be difficult. On the other hand, if you perceive that you are going to have fun, you are more likely to enjoy life as it unfolds itself to your expectations.

The law of attraction is based on an elementary concept. You attract what you choose to focus on. Whether you choose to think negatively or positively, it's all up to you. If you choose to focus on the positive side of life, you will attract good things your way. You will always be full of joy and abundance; you will live your life feeling energetic and ready to handle anything that comes your way. On the contrary, if you choose to focus on the negative, your life will be full of misery; you will never be happy with the people around you. Often, you will feel as though you are tired of living. Your productivity at work and home will be negatively affected. You're probably going to be the one who sees the bad in everything. All this is the product of what you want to concentrate on.

Knowing how the rule of attraction works will open the doors to success in your life. This law opens the minds to understand that we exist in a world of limitless possibilities, endless excitement, and limitless wealth. Dream about it, you will put your trust in your confidence and help alter future results. Isn't that awesome? Unfortunately, few people understand and successfully use the rule of attraction to change their lives.

Your ideas and emotions will work together to create an ideal future for you. Since you have the ability to decide what you want, you can ask for a life you've always dreamed of living. Your attention and resources should be in line with what you're hoping to attract.

How to Use the Law of Attraction

Once you realize that you are the maker of your own universe, you should start dreaming about making a better life for yourself. In this situation, you should be motivated to think positively, and your feelings determine what you desire in life.

This requires you to focus your time and energy on dreaming about the positive things you desire in life. It also means that you can consciously control your thoughts and desires as they shape what is embodied.

Ask, Believe, Receive

The Rule of Attraction tends to be a clear mechanism in which you wish for what you desire, and you will get it. However, the application process needs more than just a letter and a receipt. If it were that simple, then everybody would have a peaceful life free from stress and anxiety. So, what makes it easy and overwhelming to enforce the rule of attraction? Ask

Every day, people make appeals to the world, either intentionally or unconsciously, by their minds.

Whatever you're dreaming about is what you're focused on. This is where you've been channeling your powers. Using the rule of attraction, you should know that you must take conscious steps to control your thoughts and feelings. In this regard, you have to decide that you want something intentionally. This also demands that you live and act as though you already have what you are asking for.

Believe

To manifest what you desire in your life, it is imperative that you genuinely trust that you will get what you want. Your thoughts should show the certainty that you have to know that you're going to get what you want. Therefore, the mind should be free from questions. This is the most complicated part of the Law of Attraction.

Most people simply ask. However, they find it difficult to believe that they can get what they want. The aspect of belief diminishes when individuals realize that what they asked for takes longer to manifest than they expect. So, they turn their attention to negative thinking. They begin to convince themselves that it is impossible. Life is not easy. Such perceptions only affect what you are asking for from the universe. The worst thing is that negativity bias begins to take shape. Without realizing, they attract negativity in their lives because they simply failed to believe.

Receive

The last thing that you need to do is to receive what you were asking or hoping for. Perhaps this is the easiest part since it only requires you to position yourself in the best way through your emotions to receive your gift. Consider an ordinary situation where you are receiving a gift from your loved ones. Certainly, you express from your body language that you are happy. Emotions of love and appreciation should be evident when receiving any gift. This is how the universe expects you to receive your reward.

You should live your day feeling thankful and happy for what you already have. This is the best way to practice receiving what you want even before the world gives it to you. These emotions can also be shaped by how you choose to think. Accordingly, it is recommended that you should live mindfully by enhancing your self-awareness to stop yourself each time negative thoughts develop in your mind.

At first, it won't be an easy feat to control your thoughts and emotions. Nevertheless, it is worth noting that everything good calls for patience and practice. As such, for the law of attraction to work for you, you have to be patient. You have to keep practicing the habit of believing. Most importantly, always remember that you can create your happiness.

Anxiety; Stopping Negative Thoughts

Numerous factors cause anxiety. At times, it is caused by a combination of genetic factors and environmental factors. Fear within you can easily make you feel worried about things that haven't happened. In extreme cases, this leads to panic. Your mind can easily amplify the fears within you and make you believe that something bad will happen. In social settings, anxiety will leave you in a constant state of worry about saying the wrong thing in front of other people. Also, you might gain the assumption that other people will not like you. Such negative thoughts only prevent you from being yourself. It holds you back from living your life.

Common Thoughts in Anxious People

There are certain stressful thoughts evident in anxious people. Below are a few examples of some of these thoughts. Identifying these thoughts is helpful as it ensures that you find a way to deal with your anxiety. Examples of common thoughts in anxious people are as follows.

- "I am not good at what I do."

Anxious individuals will focus more on the negative aspects of themselves. In any setting, their minds will constantly think about their weaknesses. It will be difficult for them to reflect on their strengths and why they were chosen for a particular role in their workplace. Anxiety will make you feel as though your boss will fire you anytime, for example.

- "I am going to forget."

Have you ever felt that you were going to forget something even before the actual thing occurred? This is a sign that you are anxious. Believing that you are going to forget something simply means that you can't trust yourself. You're raising doubts in your mind that you can't remember to do something either during the day, tomorrow, or shortly.

- "Nobody likes me."

In the social media world, it is straightforward for an anxious person to conclude that people don't value them because they do not respond to their posts. This trait portrays someone who thinks too much. This is a person who is always worried about what other people might say. As a result, they will be too concerned about their social media posts and the responses they will be getting.

- "What if I am next?"

Without a doubt, we live in a world of uncertainty. You can never be sure about tomorrow. This can have an impact on your approach towards the unknown. There are times when you might be scared that the worst could happen to you at any time. In relation to this, you should understand that it is common to experience such thoughts. However, this doesn't mean that you should allow such thoughts to overwhelm you. Since you have some level of control of your thoughts, you should learn how to manage them. Living in constant worry that you might stumble any minute is no way to live.

- "My partner hasn't called, they must be mad at me."

Anxiety can also affect your relationships in many ways. Consider an ordinary example where your partner fails to call you during the day. There are many reasons why this could have happened. Maybe they were busy, or their phone was out of battery. However, your worrying nature will make you assume that your partner is upset at you for some reason. Having this perception will only ruin the beautiful relationship you share with your partner.

- "Did I leave the door open?"

Most people will worry too much about the simple things that they might have forgotten to do. For instance, you might question yourself about your door, appliances, or your light switches. You will find your mind wandering, thinking about whether or not the appliances were switched off. Doing this repeatedly will only lead to anxiety.

Judging from these ordinary examples of anxious thoughts, it is clear that overthinking can lead to anxiety. The simple truth is that you can stop yourself from thinking too much. Your partner fails to check on you, for example, there are many reasons why this could happen. Maybe they are busy at work, and that their smartphones are on silent mode. It could also be that they are in a meeting. Therefore, there is no need for you to think too much about it. Embrace the idea of taking things as they are without complicating them. Anxiety Triggers

There are numerous reasons why you will be anxious. There are certain events, experiences, or emotions which could worsen anxiety's symptoms. These elements are termed as anxiety triggers. The following is a concise look into some of the common triggers of anxiety.

Health Concerns

Health concerns can be a major trigger of anxiety. Usually, this happens after an upsetting medical diagnosis, such as chronic illness or cancer. It is common for people to be concerned about their life's direction when suffering from chronic disease. The good news is that you can live with this fear by adjusting how you think and see your life. Living an active life, for example, will prevent you from paying attention to the disease. Instead, you will appreciate what life has to offer and enjoy it.

Medications

Certain pills can also make you feel anxious. This is because these medications have active ingredients that affect how one feels. Common medications that could cause anxiety include weight loss medications, birth control pills, and congestion medications.

Caffeine

Caffeine can worsen or trigger the symptoms of anxiety. With a social anxiety disorder, in particular, it is advisable to lower your caffeine intake.

Skipping Meals

There are instances where you may feel jittery because of skipped meals. This happens because of the drop in your blood sugar. Eating a balanced diet is recommended for numerous reasons. It is worthwhile to strive to eat a healthy diet regularly to ensure that your body gets all the nutrients it requires. Filling yourself up with healthy snacks helps to maintain your blood sugar levels. Therefore, it reduces the likelihood of you feeling nervous or agitated.

Negative Thinking

Thinking negatively will likely corrupt your mind with feelings of frustration. This means that you are likely to feel anxious since you worry too much about the worst that can happen.

Financial Concerns

It is daunting to prevent yourself from thinking too much about your finances with the harsh economic times. This becomes a major complication when you have debts to pay, and everything appears out of hand. To deal with triggers relating to finances, you should consider seeking professional assistance. Stress

For instance, when missing important deadlines, you will worry about the potential loss of something important. You could end up developing a fear of losing your job. Indeed, this will stress you out a lot. In some cases, stress can hurt the quality of your sleep. This worsens your situation as anxiety tends to worsen when you don't have enough sleep.

Destructive Thinking; A Common Cause of Stress

Negative thinking will often lead to stress. When you constantly dwell on negative self-talk, this is what your subconscious mind will focus on. Instead of ruminating on how bad things seem to follow you, it is vital to realize that such thoughts can hurt your emotional wellbeing. To comprehend how our thoughts lead to stress, let's consider how stress works.

How Stress Works

Psychologist Albert Ellis proposed the ABC model of understanding how stress works. According to this model, external events (A) do not trigger emotions (C). However, beliefs (B) can cause emotions. This means that their external environments do not directly influence people's emotions, but they are affected by how they process what happens around them.

Arguably, stressors will always be there. For instance, getting stuck in traffic is a common thing. It only leads to stress when you handle it negatively. In this regard, having a pessimistic view about traffic will cause anxiety and stress. Recognizing that you have the power to control how you think should help you recognize that you can easily evade stress. Why should you fuss about a traffic jam when you are certain that there is nothing you can do about it? To effectively deal with such a situation, you should keep your mind engaged with something else. Listen to your favorite music as you wait for traffic to open up. Alternatively, you can listen to positive affirmations to warrant that your mind doesn't slip into negative thinking.

Stress and Negative Self-Talk

Self-talk is the inner voice that talks to you. Depending on how you use self-talk, it becomes a make or breaks the situation. Positive self-talk will remind you of the great things that you can achieve. It will help you approach life with optimism. Negative self-talk, on the other hand, will attract negative energy. You will pay too much attention to the possibility of all the bad things that could happen to you. Negative self-talk will not help you overcome the stress that you might be going through. In fact, it worsens the situation as you will feel more stressed.

Clearly, overthinking can affect your life in many ways. Whether you feel anxious, stressed, or unmotivated, all these can be attributed to how you think. Thinking positively can attract good

177

things to you. The law of attraction will always apply to your thoughts and emotions. It is through these thoughts that you create the world that you want. Negative thinking breeds negativity in your life. It will affect your relationships, work-life, and your productivity in varying aspects. Instead of worrying about the future, you should use your energy to focus more on what you can do today for a better tomorrow. Frankly, your actions determine your future. Hence, thinking alone is just not enough. You need to act.

Chapter 11: How to declutter your mind

Decide Where to Start

Most people often are tempted to begin their decluttering and organization from cabinets and drawers underneath the sink and in the hallway. While this is okay, it is even more effective and efficient to start with visible areas. Begin with a small task. Select the least used and least cluttered room first. Decluttering is traumatic because it means letting go. When you start with the least cluttered room, it will reduce the traumatic nature of your task. It's less threatening. When you conducted "Clutter Patrol" in the first preliminary exercise, you cleared out and returned your things to their rightful places. For instance, you identified all the things on the countertops, desktops, and tablets that are not necessary or are not supposed to be located here and put in the right rooms. However, you may have sadly discovered that there was "leftover stuff" for which there was no room. There were also larger objects that now occupy precious floor space. Those uncomfortable items will be relegated to the later stages of your plan. Now you can move on to shelves, countertops, drawers, closets, and cabinets. Begin from the door and work clockwise throughout the room. Techniques for decluttering will be discussed next. Always ensure that you pay close attention to one room at a time.

It is usually good to start with the least used room first, then move on to the next room that's used less often, and so on. The "Konmari" approach is somewhat different sequentially.

Whichever method you choose depends on your personality and cleaning style.

The Four-Box Technique

Find four boxes and a large magic marker. Bring them into the room you chose to start with. This means that you set out four boxes. One is for trash; the second is dedicated to selling, the next for donations, and the last one is for stuff you plan on keeping. Label each box accordingly. Focus on visual items that are on the tops of tables and open shelves. Separate your things accordingly. Next, take your four boxes to the next room. You might find that you have already filled one of them, so you may need to start a new box to replace it.

As you put in one item after the other, ask yourself the following questions:

1.   *Is this object in good condition?*

If you have items in the broken or tattered house, you need to throw them away. At this point, while decluttering, you do not need to dedicate things to fix if they're not important. If it is something that you want to fix, ensure that you put a timeline on when you will fix it and do it. If you're never going to get around to fixing it, toss it away.

2.   If this item was broken, would I rebuy it?

Most people have been victims of purchasing things they seldom or never use. Although you have already spent money on them, you may not need them. Those are things you might resell or simply toss out.

3.   Do I have one of these already?

How many hair dryers do you need? How many tables do you need in the sitting area? All these questions, and more, are the stuff that you need to take into account before decluttering seriously. You might think it's easy to get rid of all these duplicated items. It's not! Only some of the items that aren't in bad condition may be sold at a garage sale. You can make some extra money on those, and you have a box for that. Other items have no resale value and deserve to be thrown out or donated.

4.   Is this item worth saving?

Many, many things may look attractive or useful. That ratchet set is in an attractive case, and none are missing. However, if you bought it for temporary usage, why save it? It might now sell well. Besides, do you have sufficient closet or shelf space for it? Probably not.

5.   Have I used this item for the last six months?

If you have gone for six months without using something, then there is a high probability that you won't ever need it! That is for resale or disposal. So toss it into the appropriate box.

6.   *Are these "just in case" items?*

When you are working on the first two rooms, you will discover the truth about your sense of security. As you categorize items, you may catch yourself thinking that you need to keep certain items "just in case" you need it for _____ someday. You may also note that these objects are usually inconsequential and inexpensive to buy. Rethink the issue and categorize accordingly.

7.   *Do these things fit into my future vision of life?*

This is the most important question of them all. It is true that people often talk themselves into many things and even weasel their way around that question many times. However, you need to make a decision, keeping in mind your firm commitment to declutter. You have to weigh whether your choice is wise enough and in line with the vision you have for your family and home.

The truth of the matter is that no single reason can justify keeping clutter in the house. Therefore, if what you have are junky things, unnecessary duplicates, tattered or even broken items, decide to get rid of them by selling them, donating them, or discarding them.

Turn your house into a home! Ensure that the things you keep in your home are not only safe for you but also safe for your family, your guests, and your pets. People should feel comfortable and at ease whenever they are in your home. Keep your focus on your family and friends, rather than on material possessions that don't matter at all. Even your pets will demonstrate their comfort. Having friendlier surroundings has a tranquil effect on animals.

Be happy, healthy, safe, and free. Do not allow staff to control you. The only way to attain this is by living a clutter-free life forever.

The Time Segment Technique

During your house tour, you took note of the most cluttered room. Designate a time of about five minutes to a half-an-hour. Make up a "to-do list" for decluttering that room. Some rooms may require movement from section to section. It might be your office area or den. There are piles there, even though this is a digital world.

If you work mostly online, you are acutely aware of the junk files you've managed to create. Take that thirty minute time and clean up one folder after another. As each folder is finished, rename it, so you will recall which ones have been completed and which ones still need attention. *Reboot your computer after you've completed each time segment. That will help you avoid computer slowdowns and frozen screens. Haven't you had the experience of hearing an apology from a clerk you've contacted to the effect that their computers are "slow today?" That's because they failed to clean up and reboot.

The Trash Bag Approach

This is a two-bag approach.

1.   The Disposables

As you rummage through your most cluttered room (including drawers and closets), you will come upon items that definitely should be disposed of. Rather than piling up twenty bags of garbage and trudging the load out to the end of your driveway on trash day, you can decide on placing one or two additional bags out in addition to your regular disposables. This, of course, is longer-term but will save the money of having to hire a junk service. Those can become very expensive.

2.   The Giveaway's

Research online and locate charity groups that will pick up items from you. Don't think about whether or not this is a "legitimate" charity. Someone who wants your stuff is going to benefit.

3.   The "Turnaround."

Because you have designated your disposables and giveaway items, you have changed your attitude. It is barely noticeable when it occurs but stands out after you've disposed of or gave away some of your stuff. You have learned how to send away some material objects. What's more, you have noticed that your house now seems cleaner and neater. It was an enjoyable feeling, wasn't it? Try it again!

Return to the rooms in your house. Search inside your drawers. Ask yourself yet again why you decided to keep each of those items. You will quickly realize that parting with the other items makes you feel better about yourself. It also strengthened your decision-making abilities. There are psychological rewards for this freeing behavior.

Again, decide whether or not each of the things in your drawers and closets is useful. Decide which ones bring you a sense of joy and are respected. Organize them neatly. Regarding clothing, ask yourself which ones deserve to hang up and which ones should be stored in drawers. Use the "roll-up" method of storing articles of clothing. Roll them up and stand them up vertically. Do not hesitate to leave space. Compliment yourself for having such a luxury.

The 12-12-12 Challenge

Make this challenge a part of your routine. This means that you ensure that you locate 12 items to throw away each day, 12 to give up to charity, and 12 to be taken back to their rightful position or into the rooms in your house. This challenge can be an enjoyable and exciting way to organize 36 items within a short duration. *Be sure to throw away, give away, or neatly store the items you have separated. Do it fast before you change your mind!

Repeat this process until there are empty areas in your drawers and on the tops of furniture. The exercise of purging is uplifting. What's more, it will make it easier to clean and polish.

Exercise for Closet and Drawer Decluttering:

Start by hanging all your clothes and jewelry in the reverse direction. Once you have worn them, put them back into the closets and drawers in the right direction. Once 4-6 months elapse, if you have not used some things at all, those are the items you need to discard or sell at a garage sale. Don't save ill-fitting clothes. Don't save clothes that are torn with the intention that you will sew them later. "Later" never happens.

Note: *Costume jewelry is valuable.* While you seldom may have worn the pin Aunt Jessie gave you, other people may find it quite attractive. If you don't want to sell it yourself or live in an area where costume jewelry is of little interest, you can always find resellers and dealers who anxiously crave it. Regardless of the distance involved, many of them will rush to your house to buy it!

The "Konmari" Method

This method is the most drastic of all and takes a lot of courage. If you have built up enough annoyance when you make your initial house tour, you will feel bound and determined to succeed with your decluttering process... If that matches your mindset, you will want to choose this approach.

1.   Start with a room that is only moderately used. (No! Definitely not the kitchen!)

2.   Choose to attack a closet, a cabinet, or half of the drawers in a dresser.

3.   Throw everything on the floor!

4.   Neatly put back items that you use constantly. Don't include items that you feel you may or may not use in the next six months.

5.   Grab three boxes. Label them "Trash", "Undecided," and "Give Away." Make decisions on your items, and place them in the boxes or back in the closet or drawers.

6.   Move to the next closet, cabinet, or set of drawers you want to tackle and do the same until you are done.

7.   Continue to the next room, which you use a little more often. Do up your three boxes as before. Continue to the next room until about half the rooms are categorized in the boxes, and items of use are put away.

Halfway through your house, collect the items labeled "Trash" and put them into your garbage pails. Avoid second-guessing.

---

8.   Return to the room with the undecided boxes. Now it's time to decide! Be firm, and separate that which really deserves to be trashed. Add that to your garbage pails. Pull out those useful things to give away, and move them into your "Give Away" box. If you really, really feel you need an item or two to keep, try to limit the number of saved items. Put them away neatly.

9.   Now, in those first few rooms, clear off the tops of your furniture. It's

a relief to see an empty tabletop, doesn't it? Take some time to rejoice in that feeling. It is good for your emotional well-being.

10.   Clean the tops of the furniture and polish if appropriate. Now choose just a few items to place on top. The rest can go to charity or family and friends.

_____

_____

Now you are ready for the heavily used rooms. Those rooms are usually the kitchen, the mudroom, the home office, and den if you have one. You will need to allocate more time to those rooms, obviously.

_____

_____

11.   The Infamous Kitchen

1.   A glance at your countertop. Assess the number of appliances you have stored on top, noting that some aren't used that often. However, before you can put them in your cabinets, you will have to create room for them there. Therefore, work the kitchen from the inside out – one cabinet at a time, starting with the lower cabinets. On the floor, separate the items into "always used," "used a few times a month," and "hardly ever used" and "used once or twice the past year."

In two boxes, separate the "hardly ever used" from the "used once or twice." Continue with the next lower cabinet and do the same. When you've finished with those boxes, temporarily put the "hardly ever used" and the "used once or twice in the past year" into another room.

2. Now, do you have room for those extra appliances cluttering your countertop? If so, decide as to whether or not you are going to save them. Then place the ones you want to keep in the spaces in your lower cabinets. Add the "always used" items and the "used once or twice" items.

3. Repeat the same procedure with your upper cabinets.

4. Return to the items you placed temporarily in the other room. Decide if you need them. They are the items marked "hardly ever used" and "used once or twice in the past year." Dispose of accordingly.

*Note: By the time you reach this stage, you will be taking more drastic measures to get rid of unneeded items and reducing clutter.

12. The Mud Room

The mudroom is easier, despite the dirt and leaves that were dragged in from outside. Clean off the boots. Examine the jackets and coats, return them to their rightful places in the house, or throw it into the laundry if needed. You will note that many items are duplicates. Perhaps some of ready for the trash Clean the mudroom floor. That is a gratifying experience, and you will want to take the time to admire the results of your efforts.

13.   The Home Office and Den

Yes, the office! That will take a while if you take a lot of work home from your job or have a side business. By the time you decide to declutter, you will realize that you've accumulated many trinkets and containers stuffed with riff-raff. Those have little to do with your work, so start on the first. Desks should have a lot of space for your daily tasks. Some people have a lot of paper files stored in file cabinets or desk drawers. Once you go through them, you may discover that they contain many antiquated items that need to be thrown into the recycling bin. Sometimes entire files are no longer needed. Once you've cleared all that out, you may find out that you need far less space.

If you use a computer that appropriately has a "desktop." If it's a jumble, return the misplaced folders to your documents or other specific areas you've designated. Next, go through the tedious task of straightening out your folders. Attack the moderately used folders first and trash the excesses. Then move to the moderately used folders and do the same. *Reboot your computer. Otherwise, your activity will slow your computer down to a crawl. Last to attack are your often-used and current files. You may need to create new file folders for those. By now, you'll have more room for them, if needed.

Note: Take some time to explore your hard disk file, open up your applications directory, and eliminate all those pesky extra games and the like that you aren't likely to use at all. Those are usually the ones that came with your computer when you purchased it.

For your den or that of your spouse, create a more utilitarian and fun area. Rearrange furniture to be conducive to the various functions it serves. Perhaps that might mean creating a little conversational area, or an area for watching TV and playing video games, or an area for music. Then there are areas designated for a dartboard, a pool table, or card table, for example. Different types of lighting will be needed in each of those areas. Maybe there's an extra lamp in another room of little use.

The "Drop Zone"

Every house has a "drop zone." That's a haphazardly selected area where your family puts the mail, where the children put their backpacks and leftover lunches, where you and your spouse dropped the car keys, and all sorts of junk. Designate a better area for those things. Of course, food items and backpacks don't belong in the "drop zone" at all. Encourage members of your family to cooperate in that effort. Most people would prefer to procrastinate so that it might become an important family rule. Although it takes a little extra time and effort to execute that thankless task, it will eliminate early morning panics when someone can't find something. A cluttered "drop zone" is also the reason why some folks are late with invoices. (They get mixed up with the other clutter!) Invoices should be put in a designated area on your desk. If you have room, sometimes a card table or small tall table can serve the role of a "drop zone," rather than the kitchen table, by the way!

A word about containers

Some professionals recommend that you don't use containers in which to pack your clothes or cabinet items. Certain types might be helpful, although others might not be. Be very selective when you choose containers. There are some types of clothing hangers sold that hold a multitude of dresses or pants. They are not recommended for three reasons:

1.   You will be tempted to save far too many clothes.

2.   Your clothing will get wrinkled up because everything is being crushed together.

3.   The weight may be too heavy, and the dowel in your closet will bend.

Avoid the temptation of stacking plastic containers one on top of the other on your closet shelf. Eventually, you will need a step stool or even and ladder to reach the ones on top!

Installing smaller shelves in your closet may be very helpful. Most of those shelves aren't designed to hold a lot of excess sweaters, shirts, etc. That will help you trim down the amount of clothing you keep.

Containers that are stored in your bed are not recommended. They are inconvenient and gather dust bunnies!

Do you ever feel affected by all the things you're hanging on to? It is difficult to get organized? Do you feel like your life is packed with obligations, things, relationships, or even a career that doesn't fit the person you have grown to become?

Deliberately discovering who you are now and where you want to go with your life can allow you to cut through all the clutter and create an environment and a lifestyle that feels comfortable with the best parts of you.

Releasing the things that no longer rhyme with the person you have grown into helps you in so many different parts. Not only is it easier to remain organized when you have fewer things in your life, but the act of purging can also allow you to re-evaluate what is critical to you and achieve better clarity about your values.

The more we have on our plate, the less energy and attention we have for any activity — deep engagement results in happiness and enjoyment. A scattered mind is not a happy mind.

Decluttering doesn't just create happiness, but it improves performance as well. When we choose to declutter our lives often, it's because we hope for some kind of order, some peace or even some relief from inner and outer chaos. Something transformational always happens when we get into the process of decluttering. We begin to discover ourselves. And if we proceed with it on levels, decluttering can be become a place of deep growth.

Decluttering makes us confront some major relationships we have to our things and the world around us. We discover that clutter normally represents procrastination and denial patterns, and if we are to focus on the clutter, we must change those patterns. We start to understand how much weight we place on objects. Our belongings can provide us with a sense of identity. They can provide us with a sense of security or comfort. They represent our hope for the future or memories. But as we discover our connections to things, we also learn how to let go. This requires a lot of mindfulness, and the realization that we have happiness within us and letting go of objects is an act of that realization.

One of the best things about decluttering is that it forces you to ask a great question:

What is Significant to Me?

As you deal with a pile of clothes, a shelf overflowing with books, a cluttered desktop, there's no way to eliminate clutter without answering that question. To toss anything out, you have to consider what you feel is important and what isn't. Simplicity involves identifying what's critical and letting go of the rest.

This is when you hit the required question of what you value the most. Some examples of this include:

Loved ones

Service

Meaningful work

Healthy life

When you start to become conscious of your values, something wonderful happens, you begin to live in alignment with those priorities.

Organization in the Workplace

Having an organized workplace free of clutter and inviting can easily simplify your day, giving you the inner and outer space to complete more tasks and free yourself from stress generating distractions. If you've put off correcting the mess because of some reason, or you don't just have the energy to make choices about your things, here's the way out.

Do yourself a favor and remove all the junk and unnecessary possessions that add value to your life. These are items that you own that limit negative emotions and destroy your emotional well-being.

1. Clean out one place at a time

The first step to decluttering is to clean out your living room. Yes. Deep clean your living space. It might sound daunting and onerous to declutter all the junk in your living quarters, but here is a simple hack to get it done.

Rather than try to go through your whole apartment or house at once, just select one area, and clean it. Clean the area thoroughly and keep some items there.

In most cases, when you try to clean an entire house, you will skip some places or sections. But, when you focus on one area at a time, you shouldn't miss any spots.

When you're going through your stuff, if you find yourself thinking that you may need to use a certain item in the future and it has been sitting there untouched, throw it away.

Be Choosy on What You Allow Into Your Life

Now that you have removed some items out of your life, it is important to be selecting what you let into your life.

Think long and hard about the relevancy the item will bring to your day-to-day life. Hopefully, you will realize that really, you don't need a lot to live your life, and all this superfluous thing is harsh to your health.

Being choosy on what you allow into your life will allow you to avoid getting into the vicious cycle of reorganizing things you never use. Break the cycle of "organizing" and "decluttering" just to own a lot of things by being selective on what you want to allow back into your life.

Cleaning up Your Life

Decluttering doesn't involve throwing things out. Decluttering is more about establishing an environment that promotes productivity, happiness, and peace of mind in your life. In the end, your happiness and peace of mind are all that is important. A lot of clutter can represent a lack of control. And the most worrying thing is the kind of clutter that can block the neural networks. This form of clutter will be slower and less efficient in processing information.

In general, clutter can negatively affect your work, health, performance, and possibly even your relationships.

Techniques to Declutter Your Life, Eliminate Stress and Clear Your Mind

1. Develop a decluttering checklist

Decluttering is a major problem for many people, probably because of fear. Suppose I throw away that pair of pants and regret that decision even if they were uncomfortable, and I disliked them? What if I need to fix a problem someday, but I deleted the manual? You get what I mean.

One way to eliminate fear is to understand that removing the clutter from your life doesn't mean living a life without any items you like. You'll be decreasing the number of things you own? For instance, do you want to have a closet full of blankets? You probably need one lighter one for when it's warm and thicket comfort for the colder seasons.

To assist you in getting started, develop a decluttering checklist. It can simplify this process and provide you a visual representation of what you need to be cut down.

2. Does it create joy?

If you know Marie Kondo, then you should know this tip. However, for those who don't know her, it's pretty simple.

Anytime you're cleaning your workplace or home, physically touch the item that you're deciding about. Next, ask yourself the following question, "does it trigger joy?" Well, it's not a must to ask that literally. But, the point here is to reflect on what you feel as you hold the object. For instance, Kondo didn't want to discard an old and ragged t-shirt from an event she attended because when she held the shirt, it rekindled good memories.

What if the object doesn't trigger such feelings? Then you should part ways with it.

3. Apply a no-freebies policy

We've all been in this state before. You attend a conference and come with a ton of free swag.

It might appear like a good idea at first. However, the truth is more stuff adding into your clutter-and its stuff you really don't need. While this definitely requires some will power, you should avoid accumulating these freebies.

4. Don't overwhelm yourself, start small

Let's be honest here. How likely are you going to organize and clean your whole home, office, or life in one day? That would be so ambitious it would tire you and possibly prevent you from ever getting started.

Instead, take small steps. Probably set aside five minutes every day to pave the way a small area like a desk drawer or your car. After setting up some momentum, set aside more time. Commit one afternoon to get your office back in order.

5. Perform a calendar audit

Clutter doesn't entail the items taking up physical space. It can also be the entries you have included in your calendar. Typically, a calendar audit involves minute activities and anything you do automatically, like brushing your teeth. Other examples would be irrelevant meetings and recurring events that no longer fit into your schedule.

Check your calendar and remove these tasks and events from it. Moving forward, start saying "yes" to less and use a scheduling assistant. You need to also share your calendar with others to avoid double bookings and scheduling conflicts.

6. Unsubscribe and remove

Trying to stay up to date with your inbox is a waste of time. It's a distraction that is affecting your productivity and eating into your happy life. With that in mind, one of the easiest means to deal with your inbox is to unsubscribe from the emails that you never read. The same idea applies to magazines and newspapers that you never opened.

7. Automate

Here's a simple method to clear your mind; automate. Examples include scheduling social media posts or setting out-of-office auto-responder emails.

8. Create a social event

Sometimes, it's interesting to do fun things with others. And that is fun when it comes to decluttering.

Apart from spending time with your family or friends, they can also help you know what to throw away and what to keep. Just remember to return a favor.

9. Try mindfulness

One of the best methods to clear your mind and decrease stress and anxiety is to try mindfulness meditation. Why mindfulness works is because it redirects your attention and thoughts to the present. You will stop being consumed by the future, past, and negative self-talk.

10. Simplify your goals

It is important to set goals. Goals direct you on what you need to do and allow you to monitor your progress. But, targets are only useful if you have established a small number of specific goals and objectives.

Revise your goals to ensure that they're not too broad or unrealistic. From there, create a plan on how you'll follow through with them. Write down your steps if you might need to do it.

11.   Get rid of toxic people from your life

Evaluate all the people in your life. And then, keep off from people who are not worth the time and energy.

12.   Unplug and unwind

Your brain deserves time to recharge and rest. This will help you to become more productive and less depressed.

Schedule constant breaks throughout the workday and get away momentarily. Unwinding your mind allows you to cut down the amount of media that you take in. Overall, you want to discover new information and skills. However, a lot of it can block your brain.

Declutter Your Key Values

Step 1: Highlight Your Core Values

To understand why certain things are wrong, you must develop a strong grasp of what is right for you.

What do you want to be, and how would you want to live your life?

If you have never listed your values, you are living a life without a compass. You're letting the winds and storms define where you need to go and accept the results without question. Even if you have defined them for a long time, it doesn't hurt to revisit them because your values can change over time.

Once you have created a list of values that match your goals, re-evaluate them daily, and ensure that the actions you take match the desired results. You may want to concentrate first on your personal values and then on your professional values. Or you might select one value from each and start there.

Regardless of what you select, make sure you start with the area of your life where you feel there is a huge disconnect. This is the point where you feel the most internal pain and mental agitation. Revise your action list daily so that you can make changes and boundaries that limit you from mindlessly wandering away from your values again.

Even small changes can create a massive, positive change in your attitude. You'll develop a sense of direction and purpose that appears authentic to you, even if you can't act on it right away. This is a huge feeling.

Still, you will have moments of transition and challenges, but these practices will offer you tools to overcome all the obstacles in life.

Step 2: Define Your Life Priorities

Once you have outlined your key values, these values will help you complete an exercise that will improve your life. Define your life priorities so that you can spend your time, money, and energy.

Without understanding our priorities, we let the pressure of life to guide our actions and decisions. An attractive offer comes, and we purchase it. Someone interrupts our workflow, and we permit it. When we don't know the bigger "why" of our lives, there are no boundaries to help us.

Below is an exercise to help you determine where you are spending money, energy, and time.

How much time per day do you think you waste on irrelevant activities not connected to your main values?

How are you connecting with people you care about unconsciously?

How do you make life decisions?

How are you using money unconsciously?

What obligations, tasks, and connections are you letting in your life unconsciously?

How are you neglecting other critical parts of your life that you tend to have no time for?

Now that you have a vague idea of how much you are using your energy and concentration let's explore the right way you'd like to prioritize your life's critical areas.

Let's look at seven sections of your life that will help you determine your priorities and how you want to use time and money.

If you want to eliminate any of these areas, please do so if they don't apply to you.

The areas of your life include:

1. Family

2. Marriage

3. Self-improvement

4. Leisure

5. Life management

6. Career

7. Health and fitness

If you sleep 8 hours a day, you are going to be left with 16 waking hours. Now, let's set aside 2 hours for personal hygiene activities and eating. Then you will be left with 14 hours. In a week, that translates to 98 hours per week.

In a typical world, how can you prioritize those seven areas of your life? How many hours in a week are you ready to commit to each sector?

It's good to start with the priority to make the most positive difference in your life or where you feel the most imbalance. You might find this section reflecting one or more of your values that you aren't honoring.

For instance, you may have a core value associated with family and life priority of spending enough time with your family. Start small by deciding to include an extra hour a week spending time with your family.

Of course, this will affect some other tasks, but you should ensure it affects tasks that are not a big priority.

Keep adding weekly time to your life priorities until you have them reorganized to match your ideal.

Sometimes, altering a priority can be hard. If you want to spend more time with your kids and wife, it will affect your work schedule? If yes, what do you need to take charge of any fallout?

If you want to concentrate more on your health and fitness, you will need to develop challenging habits to follow through on this priority.

If you want to experience a healthy marriage, you might need to give up time in front of the TV or the computer, which might be hard at first.

Simply defining your life priorities isn't enough. You need to take the difficult actions necessary to make the changes you want to see in your life. However, the closer you come to your real goal, the less internal battles you will feel.

As time goes, you won't miss those old habits, behaviors, and choices. Your life will flow more easily because you are living authentically, true to your priorities and values.

Step 3: Concentrate on Mindful Goal Setting

A natural result of setting priorities and having values is thinking about how they apply to your life in the future. While worrying about the future leads to an unsettled mind, planning for the future is a critical and valuable aspect that can set the stage for true satisfaction for the years to come.

Well, it's possible to look forward to a better future and remain happy with your life right now? Can you be satisfied and change at the same time? We know it's possible to concentrate on the future while still learning how to enjoy the current moment.

The realities of our lives are constantly pushing us into the future. We are anxious about paying the bills, how our children will turn out whether we will remain healthy. And the way of setting goals is future-oriented.

Longing and fighting against what causes suffering. Hoping for more, for something different, for something better at the expense of contentment in the current status denies us of life.

But remember that change will come whether or not you choose to focus.

Change is a must, whether we are sitting or wringing our hands about some imagined future results. So we might as well define our futures mindfully.

Once you acknowledge the truth that contentment and change can take place simultaneously, you decrease the tension between wondering it's an either-or proposition. There's a means to create a balance between self-creation and mindfulness.

You can check the process of creating and fulfilling your goals as a place for happiness and contentment. Instead of holding back happiness while you wait for a result, enjoy every stage along the path. Every small effort toward your goals should be celebrated.

Let's see how to create and strive toward your goals in a manner that supports the bigger "why" of your life.

When you first sit down to focus on your future goals, bear in mind that your core beliefs and life preferences are useful as a reference point. As long as your beliefs and objectives remain true, they should be a guide to your goals. If not, brace yourself for the future of regret and unhappiness.

Step 4. Define SMART Goals

The easiest way to focus on what is important in life is to define SMART goals.

Set goals for each quarter instead of a yearlong goal that usually takes you out of the current moment.

Your goals should be Smart, Measurable, Achievable, Relevant, and Time-bound.

Step 5: Connect Goals to Your Passions

Most people live desperate lives. They wake up with a low-level sense of anxiety. At work, they feel underrated and undermined. And when they arrive home, they feel physically and mentally tired, with just enough energy to cook, take care of the family, and spend a few hours watching television. Then they sleep and wake up to do the same thing.

While this may not describe you exactly, you can still relate. We all accept less than our dreams. We remain in jobs that don't motivate us or make us happy. All this adds to our mental clutter.

Life has a means of eating us, and before we discover, we're already far down a path that doesn't look what we want for our lives. By the time we discover it, we have duties that add another reason to maintain the status quo-even if we hate it.

The fact is that your mental health can be destroyed when you feel unsatisfied with your work. Consider the amount of negative mental energy you have subjected to a bad boss or a career move you regret. We spend a lot of time working. Therefore, the decision you make about your job will have the ability to make or break your general happiness.

If you get a job that you love, not only will this free your mind from oppressive thoughts but will also feel energized in parts of your life.

Well, What Does it Mean to Live Your Passion?

It can be defined using a few examples.

You have a high sense of self-confidence and motivation about what you're doing because it is best for you.

You feel like you are in the best place, doing something in your work or life that feels authentic to who you are and how you're wired.

Your entire life is better, and your relationships are happier because you are more self-directed and present in your work.

You attract interesting, like-minded people in your life and work.

Discovering your true passion and making it part of your life isn't something that takes place overnight. It is not like teaching you how to follow a recipe or drive a car. It involves different actions and experiments to figure everything out.

Conclusion

Decluttering your life allows you to live a better-quality life. Because you have taken away the unnecessary baggage that you have been carrying around in your life, most times, all this baggage may be oblivious to you, but you are feeling its effects. Some of them cause poor health and a lack of growth in your life.

Everyone wants to grow in their life. We all want to achieve our goals and have success. I am yet to meet someone that does not want to experience the joy of being associated with success because of something good that they did. I usually have mental pictures of someone giving me a medal and putting it around my neck every time I achieve.

You have been brave to choose to declutter your life. But you will be even braver if you implement in your life all that you have learned in the chapters above. Remember that the process of decluttering your life is unique to everyone.

The way one person does it may not benefit you. It is important to find ways that work for you as you do this. To make sure you get the full benefits of your life, just as you're messing around with the rules of a diet to find the ideal match.

Start by having a schedule. Do not go into your day blindly and have all the tasks and activities of the day hitting you head-on. A schedule will keep you organized. It will help you make sure that you are working on all your important tasks and giving them the attention they need.

Decluttering your life will lead you to a life of financial freedom. You will stop spending your money on unnecessary items and ventures that make no sense in your life. You will start living your life with intention. All that you purchase will be a need that is coming in to improve your life quality.

You will become more intentional with your savings and investments. Now that you have enough money to save, you can invest in assets to bring you more money. As long as you invest in a good asset and take care of your investment, it will always fetch you more money. And good money for that.

Remember that no one will hire you and pay you one billion dollars. It is your efforts and how you use the resources that are available to you that will get you there.

Keep good friends that are genuinely in your life because they love you. Not people that are in constant competition with you and are working to bring you down. A friend is someone that waters your garden to help in your growth. And it would be best if you watered theirs too.

When everyone in the group is winning, then your friendship will be more enjoyable. It is not fair to have people in the group suffering, yet you can help them grow and attain their success. That of others will not undermine your own success. Rather it will be more relevant and uplifted. Because two heads are better than one, and you will all be able to sit and talk about ways to grow even more.

Toxic friendships are draining and need to be eliminated from your life fully. Be very careful about who you are letting into your life. Let them be people who will accept you for who you are and are constantly working to help you become better.

It is important to your life and your health that you unplug and take time to rest. This is the time your mind and body take to recharge. And you will be able to think better about your plans. I find myself coming up with better plans when I am relaxed. My mind can think out of the box and explore other options and new ways of doing things.

When the mind is tired, it only thinks of things that are common to it. But when you have rest, you can think more and out of the box. You can expand your territories and not limit yourself. And your plan will be amazing, and it will lead you to good and successful results.

Your mental and physical health is also protected because you are not allowing yourself to reach burnout. Your body and mind are getting the rest they require before they start working, robotically and on autopilot mode.

The need to make assertive decisions has been analyzed. You need to get away from decision fatigue because you are overwhelmed by all the decisions you have to make in a day. And your decisions should be made assertively in ways that people understand them and respect them.

Stick to the new schedule you created for yourself when you decluttered your life. Because right now, your mind has no baggage. And you are in the best shape you can be, meaning that you are achieving a lot.

Your success, health, and growth matter a lot. Never undermine them for temporary pleasures that bring no positive impact on your life.

Let me say just one more thing!

This concludes this book on decluttering.

I hope it was a good read: I tried to cover all the aspects necessary to understand how to free yourself from the chaos around and live a new, peaceful, and more productive life.

In summary, we tried to understand which are the most frequent problems that cause overthinking; we also tried to list strategies capable of minimizing the negative thoughts that are most often connected anxiety and depression, as well as paralysis before action.

You should be able to think positively now.

We talked about minimalism and how important it is to minimize external clutter to bring order to your thoughts: if the external environment is messed up, how do you think you can have order in your mind?

It is not easy to switch to this totally different way of thinking and living, but I can assure you that it will bring positive things into your existence.

We also talked about the importance of habits, how to acquire new ones, and abandoning old ones.

In fact, it is often the habits that keep us anchored to our old self, the very thing we are trying to change.

Do you feel ready to embark on a new life path, lightened and determined? I wish you so.

See you next time.